LUMBER GHOSTS

LUMBER GHOSTS

•

A Travel Guide to the
Historic Lumber Towns
of the Pacific Northwest

•

Kenneth A. Erickson
Photographs by the author

PRUETT PUBLISHING COMPANY
BOULDER, COLORADO

Printed in the United States
10 9 8 7 6 5 4 3 2 1

Library of Congress Cataloging-in-Publication Data

Erickson, Kenneth A., 1934-
    Lumber ghosts : a travel guide to the historic lumber towns of the
Pacific Northwest / Kenneth A. Erickson.
        p.   cm.
    Includes index.
    ISBN 0-87108-854-1 (PB : acid-free)
    1. Ghost towns—Washington (State)—Guidebooks. 2. Ghost towns—
Oregon—Guidebooks. 3. Washington (State)—History, Local.
4. Oregon—History, Local. 5. Washington (State)—Tours.
6. Oregon—Tours. 7. Lumber trade—Washington (State)—History.
8. Lumber trade—Oregon—History. I. Title.
F892.E75   1994
917.9504'43—dc20   93-49503
                                                              CIP

Cover and book design by Jody Chapel, Cover to Cover Design

CONTENTS

PREFACE

The scenic mountains, coastlines, volcanoes, lakes, and gorges form great magnets for travel in the Pacific Northwest, but they tend to overwhelm an equally intriguing human landscape between mountain summits and seashores. The paucity of summer traffic on the lowland back roads, in comparison to the high concentration on freeways, indicates that much of the cultural flavor of the Northwest is lost to the casual tourist. Unfortunately, it is on these very back roads that one finds the interesting and fast-vanishing past of the Northwest—the old lumber towns, some dead, others dying.

A shard of dishware, an exotic flower, or a weathered board streaked only with paint flecks on the gray and twisted furrows, may comprise the only readily visible artifacts of past places. They remind us of places that were, of houses, children and schools, steam whistles, and daily routines. Elsewhere, the vestige of a community, a cluster of a few older houses, with no apparent reason for its remote location, represents some lingering occupation of a once larger town. Active towns with standing residences occupied, stores (some vacant), and services (some missing) may lack signs of modern construction and produce a feeling that the buildings are too large, overly periodized, and poorly maintained. A poshly modern shoreline development may oddly include an old railroad grade through a residential area, a few 1920s homes, and some rotting stubs of piling at water's edge. In the Northwest all of these places may be lumber ghosts.

Frankly, I wrote this book for the reader with a bent for the unusual. Whatever the motivation for a visit, be it photography, metal detection, bottle collection, or simply wanderlust, the out-of-the-way lumber towns offer an outlet for enjoyable and directed travel. The text includes detailed direction and mileage to the old sites and, if the information is available, a description of past glories and present condition. Route maps, old town plans, and photographs supplement the text.

Many people contributed to the information contained on the following pages. Anonymous writers from the 1930s collected in the *4L Lumber News* an important record of sawmilling places. People behind the counters in county assessors' offices, county engineers, museum curators, municipal and college librarians, and industry representatives each contributed information and direction to sources. I am especially indebted to the kindly folks living at the sites who volunteered their knowledge of the past. Above all, my gratitude goes to Jo Ann: wife, travel companion, note taker, mileage recorder, sandwich maker, roadsign finder, and second pair of eyes.

Lincoln City, Oregon
December 20, 1992

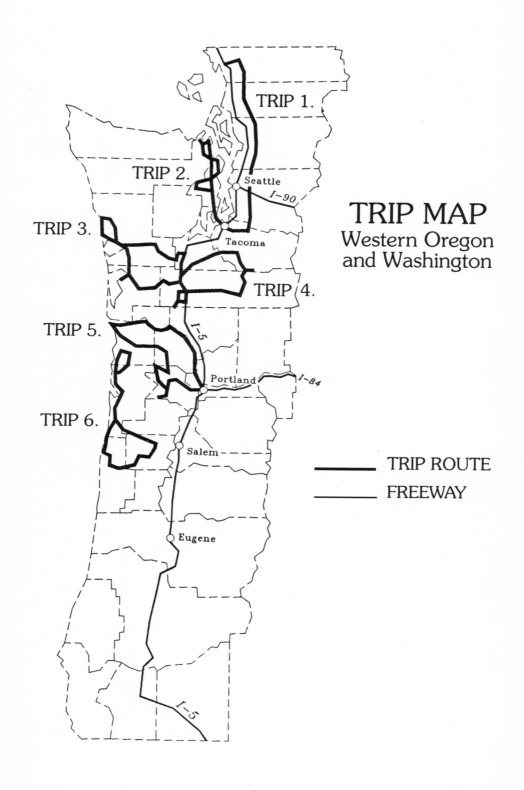

TRIP 1.

TRIP 2.

Seattle

I-90

TRIP MAP
Western Oregon
and Washington

TRIP 3.

Tacoma

TRIP 4.

TRIP 5.

I-5

Portland

I-84

TRIP 6.

Salem

TRIP ROUTE

FREEWAY

Eugene

I-5

INTRODUCTION

The epoch of lumbering in the Douglas fir region of the Pacific Northwest is fast closing. The era opened around 1850 with a few early steam sawmills at tidewater, the Oregon coast, the Columbia River, and Puget Sound. During these early decades of tidewater sawmilling, logs were cut with axes and gathered by ox team from forests adjoining waterways along which the logs would be rafted to the mills. From the big steam-powered sawmills the lumber was sent by sailing ship to Pacific ports, principally those in California.

Around the end of the nineteenth century the whole pattern of lumbering changed. Railroads opened the vast interior forests of western Oregon and Washington; crosscut saws and donkey engines sped up the logging operations; electricity powered ever bigger sawmills; logging and sawmilling companies built large camps and towns for their employees; and, with this vast shift in production scale, a new contingent of unmarried loggers and mill workers arrived overseas from Scandinavia and over the continent from cut-out forests in the Lake States and South. The southerners tended to settle cohesively in places like Darrington or Morton in Washington or Glendale in Oregon. The midwesterners, often mill owners, railroad men, and logging engineers, formed an upper managerial level in the industry. And where there was logging, there were Swedes.

The end of readily accessible private timber, with its disastrous economic result, coincided with the Great Depression of the 1930s, during which lumber company after lumber company declared bankruptcy. As the whole regional economy collapsed, strings of sawmill towns and logging camps vanished almost overnight. From 1940 through the 1950s the use of the log truck and the Caterpillar tractor brought some revitalization to the sawmilling industry, but on a scale much smaller than that of the 1920s. By 1960, the old lumbering days were fading into blurred memory. Gone were the *snus*-chewing lumberjacks, the bunkhouses, company towns, crummies, donkey engines, logging railroads,

1

An ox team and skid road in the nineteenth century. (*Courtesy Hoquiam Library*)

and, most importantly, gone, too, were the great stands of virgin timber. In their place are a few modern industrial towns supported by pulp-and-paper corporations. The extensive but diminished private forest is one composed of second-growth trees harvested periodically by industrial workers who probably live with their families in a modern house in a larger town. The public forestlands, once a storehouse of old-growth timber, are now reaching depletion and are subject to cutting restrictions stemming from ecological considerations.

On the following pages, six trips are laid out for western Oregon and Washington, the heart of the old lumbering empire. These particular routes were chosen to cover a wide sampling, and they are balanced by driving convenience and historical significance. All told, the six trips reach about eighty old lumber towns, many of which are now ghosts or in advanced stages of decay. Mileage is point-to-point (as opposed to cumulative), with the obvious advantage that any portion of a trip may be executed without burdensome mileage correction. An abbreviation used in the text follows common practice in the industry. This is the Roman numeral "M," standing for daily production in thousands of board feet, an abbreviation used repeatedly to designate sawmilling capacities: for instance, 100 M indicates a mill sawing one hundred thousand board feet per day.

The pleasure derived from the six trips depends in large measure on the reader's imagination and keenness of vision. Pack the picnic basket, keep your eyes open, and good hunting.

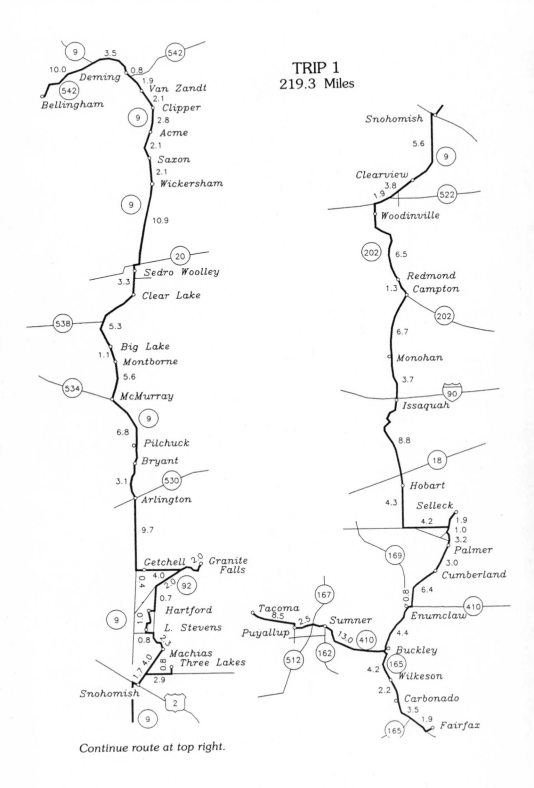

TRIP 1
219.3 Miles

Continue route at top right.

TRIP 1

BELLINGHAM TO TACOMA
(219.3 MILES)

The major portion of this north-to-south trip follows backcountry roads some twenty miles behind the urbanized shore of Puget Sound. The forest along the route has been cut over, primarily in the period from 1890 to 1930, and existing trees represent second-growth forest. The rolling hills, low ridges, and lakes, traceable to continental glacial origin, have been reworked by several large rivers flowing westward from the Cascade Mountains.

The great nineteenth-century forest behind the waters of Puget Sound provided a resource base for the longest string of old sawmilling towns in the Pacific Northwest. In this area the western red cedar (actually *Thuja*) reached its maximum size and areal extent and formed the base for a large shingle industry. Near the Snohomish River in 1893, one red cedar, its top broken at one hundred feet, measured at its base over eighty feet in circumference and twenty-seven feet in diameter. Douglas fir, the other principal timber tree of the area, sustained large-scale lumber manufacturing.

Exploitation of the vast interior forest came on the heels of railroad-building to inland points during the 1890s. One of the routes stands out—the old Seattle & International Railway (Northern Pacific), or the S. & I. for short, completed in 1890 between Seattle and the Canadian border at Sumas. Over its 127 miles of track, no less than twenty-five big sawmills were constructed in addition to a myriad of small tie and shingle mills. South of Seattle, the sawmilling picture was much the same, although slightly later in origin. All told, the railroad lumber towns reached the peak of their boom in the decade before World War I and declined rapidly after the mid-1950s. Many today are ghost towns and whistle-stops.

Itinerary

Miles	**Place**

Start   Bellingham, Washington

10.0   Bellingham to State 9 via State 542. Turn off Interstate 5 in Bellingham onto the Mt. Baker Highway (State 542). At ten miles, State 9 merges with State 542. Veer right (south) here, following State 9-542 up the narrow Nootsack Valley.

3.5   State 9-542 to Deming. For the next one hundred miles the route follows closely the old S. & I. Railway. State 9 parallels much of the original trackage; the railroad right-of-way is clearly marked by a string of brush and small trees that have grown up along the edge of the tracks.

Deming. Around 1900, Deming supported a half-dozen shingle mills in the town and along the track just outside. Today it is an agricultural and junction town.

0.8   Deming to State 542 junction. State 542 (left) leads to Mt. Baker. Continue south on State 9.

1.9   State 542 junction to Van Zandt via State 9.

Van Zandt. Where today a crossroads store stands is the only evidence of the earlier prosperous mill town of Van Zandt. C. R. Wilson's mill produced 74 M daily and supported the community of 150 persons.

2.1   Van Zandt to Clipper, State 9. Clipper, now a vacant country store and old schoolhouse, once was a small center for surrounding tie and shingle mills.

2.8   Clipper to Acme, State 9.

Acme. A residential cluster along the trackage is the remnant of the old lumber town, which maintained a saw and shingle mill.

2.1   Acme to Saxon, State 9.

           Saxon. Now but a store, Saxon was for many years a logging
           headquarters of the Bloedel Donovan Lumber Company (Belling-
           ham) before the company's move to Canada.

2.1   Saxon to Wickersham, State 9.

           Wickersham. Nestled between a rail spur and the main line, a
           small street grid over which nearly ten inhabited houses remain con-
           stitutes the town site (primarily Railroad and School avenues). Two
           hundred yards south, a road leads down to the old depot and mill
           sites.

11.0   Wickersham to Sedro Woolley, State 9. About 3.6 miles south of
           Wickersham lies Thornwood, once a small mill town. At the
           northern edge of Sedro Woolley, State 20 cuts across the edge of
           town. Turn right on State 20 and follow the highway west 0.6 miles
           to the turnoff to downtown, left (south).

           Sedro Woolley. Sedro Woolley today is not much larger than it
           was back in 1910, when it was one of the biggest towns on the
           S. & I. Railway. During the peak of the boom, the town maintained
           a resident population of three thousand persons, with ten shingle
           mills, three sawmills, and eight logging camps strung out along the
           railroads in and around Sedro Woolley. For this reason, the week-
           end crowds of mill workers and lumberjacks inflated the town popu-
           lation to the point that the business core appears to this day overly
           large for the resident population.

3.3   Sedro Woolley to Clear Lake, State 9. At the end of the main street
           of Sedro Woolley, turn right (west) on State Street 0.4 miles to
           State 9. Turn left (south) onto State 9 and, crossing the Skagit River,
           travel 2.9 miles to Clear Lake.

           Clear Lake. Sawmills here date from the 1890s (the owners were
           from Winona, Minnesota), but the big one came in 1923, when
           B. R. Lewis opened a new 300 M-capacity mill, the biggest on
           the S. & I. line. The event was attended by the governor and im-
           portant lumbermen from all over the Northwest. The auspicious

Clear Lake in 1992: the old burner stand and piling.

opening was, however, followed by a less auspicious closure due
to insolvency before the end of the decade.

A small town remains at Clear Lake, but it is only a shadow of
the old town of the early 1920s, when the population reached one
thousand persons. The site of the huge Clear Lake Lumber Company mill lies on the southern edge of town, east of the railroad
tracks and north of a pond, a site now occupied by some shops
and the Georgia-Pacific nursery maintenance headquarters. Near
the pond, the huge concrete burner stand and aging piling mutely
proclaim the past glories of the mill. The old mill office, now vacant,
stands along the roadway.

5.3   Clear Lake to Big Lake, State 9. At 3.0 miles south of Clear Lake,
State 538 intersects the main road. Turn left and continue south
on State 9 another 2.3 miles to Big Lake.

Big Lake. At the northern entry to the town, turn right to the store-
gasoline station and take the road (Lakeview Boulevard) down to
the lakeshore. The short loop south (0.6 miles) along the lake cuts

through the earlier mill town. Some company houses (modified) lie on line to the left of the roadway. Just before crossing the abandoned railroad right-of-way over to State 9, take note of where the mill once stood—to the right and below the tracks, where now stand new lakeside residences.

During the good times after 1900, Big Lake, with a company store and hotel, was the home of nearly eight hundred people, most of whom were dependent on the Day Lumber Company sawmill (100 M).

1.1 Big Lake to Montborne, State 9.

Montborne. A mile south of Big Lake on the S. & I. stood another big mill town, Montborne. The large mill (100 M per shift) of the Nelson Neal Lumber Company was located here, along with about two hundred persons.

After the mill fire of the early 1930s, the town gradually wasted away to its present skeletal form. Below and to the right of Westview Street lies the old mill site that is covered now with vines and lakeshore willows. To the east on the hillside stand a few scattered houses, two of which are rather substantial and have better withstood the deterioration of sixty years.

5.6 Montborne to McMurray, State 9.

McMurray. Today a small lakeshore resort community, McMurray was, until the Atlas Lumber & Shingle Company closed in 1923, a large mill town of five hundred persons. Along the highway in McMurray is a store–gasoline station. From here a road leads down across the tracks and back up the lakeshore (0.2 miles) to the site of the old 100 M-capacity mill. The mill site is now a small boat landing and the location of a few modular and vacation homes. Nearby stands the large abandoned home of the mill owner or superintendent. South of the store on State 9 (0.2 miles), the old town core is to be found. A private road (left) leads down to the lakeshore and the railroad tracks, where the McMurray depot once stood. To the right of the highway on the hillside are houses, occupied and vacant, and sites of others.

6.8 McMurray to Bryant, State 9. Approximately five miles south of McMurray, the highway crosses Pilchuck Creek. Along the paralleling railroad that crosses Pilchuck Creek, five hundred yards to the right and beyond a small tree farm is the site of Pilchuck.

Pilchuck. Now completely overwhelmed by vegetation, Pilchuck once was the site of the big Parker Bell Lumber Company mill (150 M), which burned down before World War I. The population in the 1890 census was 485 persons.

About 1.5 miles south of Pilchuck, State 9 bends west to recross the abandoned railroad grade.

Bryant. The logging headquarters of the Stimson Company (Seattle) was located here. A store, the abandoned headquarters building, and a few scattered houses mark the site.

3.1   Bryant to Arlington, State 9. Arlington, an active town catering to local agriculture, was once the center of the shingle industry in the heartland of western red cedar.

9.7   Arlington to Getchell Road, State 9. Turn left (east) off State 9 onto Getchell Road.

0.4   Getchell Road to Getchell.

Getchell. The main industry of Getchell before World War I was booze and prostitution. A secondary industry was the nearby collection of about a dozen tie and shingle mills. Here the famous Monte Cristo Hotel (with running water on all three floors) burned to the ground in 1893. Getchell also had the infamous Flaming Torch saloon, its name an indication of its primary service. But all the lusty past is gone and one can barely recognize a town site today: two older homes, a dilapidated church, and vacant schoolhouse.

4.0   Getchell to State 92. Continue east through Getchell, following Getchell Road to its intersection with State 92. Turn left onto State 92 to Granite Falls.

2.0   State 92 to Granite Falls. Follow the narrow and winding highway to Granite Falls.

Granite Falls. The heyday of Granite Falls goes back to a time before World War I, when the mines up the Stillaguamish River were

Getchell in 1992. This church is one of the few remaining buildings in the town site.

still producing and the Waite Mill and Timber Company, employing three hundred men, was cutting 100 M of lumber and manufacturing four hundred thousand shingles per day. During the boom years the population initially peaked around eight hundred, slumped to five hundred in 1970, and recently revived to about one thousand. Houses, box-framed, with roofs hipped to a central chimney (vintage 1910) are common in the old residential area.

5.3   Granite Falls to Machias Road junction, via State 92. Retrace west on State 92. At the Getchell Road Junction (2 miles) veer *left* and continue on State 92; 3.3 miles farther on, turn left (south) off State 92 onto Machias Road.

2.7   From State 92 to Lake Stevens. After leaving State 92, follow Machias Road 0.7 miles, then turn right (west), crossing the railroad tracks into old Hartford; follow this main roadway southward through Hartford 1.1 miles to Lake Stevens.

Lake Stevens. Lake Stevens is today a summer resort and small trading town; just after 1900 it was the booming lumber town of "Outing." The Rucker Brothers built here in 1907 a big 100 M sawmill notorious for its long working day. The sawmill burned in 1925, and during the 1930s economic woes threatened Lake Stevens with total abandonment. The town survived the critical times and now records a population higher than 1920 figures. Recent commercial development and residential expansion have made the old town almost unrecognizable.

3.1   Lake Stevens to Machias. Just through Lake Stevens, turn left (east) on 16th Street and follow the road 0.8 miles back to Machias Road. Turn right on Machias Road and proceed southward 2.3 miles to Machias.

Machias. The growth of Machias between 1894 and 1910 rivals the spectacle of its decline between 1925 and 1935. The town site was first settled by two farming families (Neimeyer and Andrus) before the building of the S. & I. Railway. In 1890 with the railroad came a New Englander, L. W. Getchell, who bought eighty

The last store on Division Street in Machias, 1992.

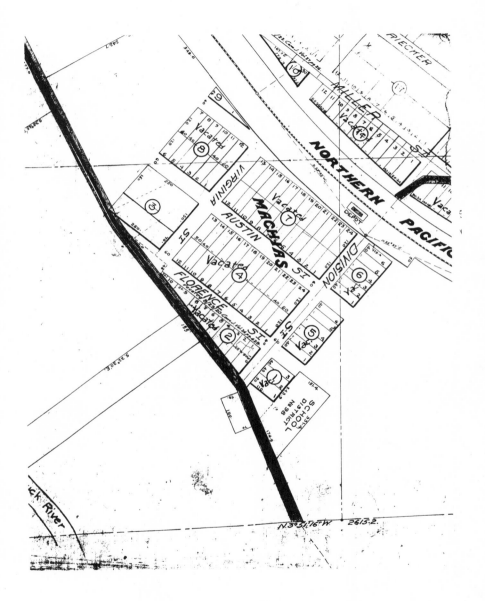

The Machias plat, now vacated.

acres from the original homesteaders, laid out a town along the tracks in the center of the Pilchuck Valley, and named the place Machias after the old sawmilling town of eastern Maine. The exact size of the town is much obscured by elapsing years, but Machias is mentioned in a 1937 report as once maintaining two steam sawmills (Bird & Pease and Andrews & Anderson) and "a dozen" shingle mills, in the late 1890s. The size of the community probably peaked between 1905 and 1910 with a population somewhere near one thousand inhabitants. At the time, Machias was large enough to justify the building of a seventy-thousand-dollar high school in the town (1907) and to support land sales within fifteen blocks of the thirty-two-block plat. In 1920 the U.S. Census indicated that the newly formed Machias Precinct contained 630 persons. By 1930 the town population had dropped to three hundred, and all the saw and shingle mills had closed. The remaining numbers in 1930 included some permanent residents (farmers), but probably also included a goodly number of loggers associated with the last-ditch clear-cutting operations of the Monroe Logging Company, which employed 250 men, gave their camp address as Machias, and maintained twenty miles of logging railroad (Western Washington Railway) out of the town. At this writing no longer a town, Machias is a small farm village containing about seventy persons.

The principal buildings of Machias are, for the most part, gone. The church still stands on its original site. The large high school, razed in the 1960s, was replaced by a district fire station. Only one false-front store survives from the line of businesses that once stretched along Division Street down from the depot (also razed). Approximately six original houses remain and stand out markedly from the few newer homes.

4.0   Machias to Three Lakes Road. Continue southward on Machias Road. At the junction four miles south of Machias, turn left (east) across the old railroad grade (now a bike path) onto Three Lakes Road.

2.9   Three Lakes Road to Three Lakes turnoff (Panther Lake Road). Turn left onto the narrow, but paved, road northward.

0.9   The road drops down to a low area before branching. This is Three Lakes.

Machias's nineteenth-century church still stands on its original site.

Three Lakes. Three Lakes, founded in 1903, lasted for twenty years and closed when the timber ran out. By the mid-1930s it was a ghost town. Three Lakes was a big place in its day—a sawmill running 150 M per shift and a town population of one thousand persons.

A combination of forest and time has removed almost all tangible evidence of the mill town. Up on the low bluff overlooking the mill site is an older and substantial home (occupied), perhaps once the home of the mill owner. At the base of the little slope is a newer home fabricated from the timbers of the old company office that stood on the same spot until the late 1960s. A few summer homes lie beyond the mill site. Otherwise, little remains. No longer do clusters of homes, stores, and the big schoolhouse (1905–1929) greet the visitor.

3.7   Three Lakes back to Machias Road. Return to Machias Road by way of entry. At the highway turn left (south) toward Snohomish.

1.7   Machias Road to U.S. 2 junction (Snohomish).

Snohomish. Snohomish was one of the earlier and more well-known lumber towns of Washington. Both logging and sawmilling were underway five years before the town was platted (1871) and well before railroad-building. By 1890 the town population reached 2,469; by 1910 Snohomish counted 3,244 persons, a goodly percentage of whom were employed in the nine sawmills or forty-two saloons of the town. In the declining years of prosperity, the much rebuilt Cascade Lumber Company plant (125 M per shift) burned to the ground in 1927. After hard Depression years, the town revived to flourish with the agricultural development of the rich Snohomish Valley soils (1990 population: 6,500).

A short loop off the main highway down to the old downtown on First Street is well worthwhile. Here a flavor of the nineteenth-century lumber town lingers. The hillside supports some fine old examples of Victorian homes.

5.6   Snohomish to Clearview, State 9. Exit Snohomish westward on U.S. 2 and turn left (south) onto State 9 just west of town.

3.8   Clearview to State 522 (freeway). Turn right (west) onto the freeway.

1.9   State 522 to Woodinville. Turn off the freeway at the Woodinville
        exit.

6.5   Woodinville to Redmond, State 202. Follow the winding road
        southward, passing the Ste. Michelle Vineyards. Proceed through
        Redmond to Cleveland Street, following it left (east) out of town.

1.3   Redmond to Issaquah turnoff, State 202. At 1.3 miles south of
        Redmond, turn right onto East Lake Sammamish Parkway.

6.7   East Lake Sammamish Drive to Monohan.

        Monohan. Once again, lakeside homes have enveloped most of
        the old mill site. Just behind a waterfront tier of lots, and shadowed
        by Lombardy poplars, lies the outline of the old mill (100 M), which
        closed in the late 1920s.

3.7   Monohan to Issaquah. Proceed southward on East Lake Sam-
        mamish Drive across U.S. 10 and into Issaquah.

8.8   Issaquah to Hobart. Follow the main street of Issaquah southward
        out of town. Stay on this paved highway, following the signs to
        Hobart. At 7.8 miles, pass under State 18. Hobart lies one mile
        beyond the underpass.

4.3   Hobart to Georgetown junction. Follow the highway through
        Hobart. Cross the Cedar River. At the junction (4.3 miles) turn
        left (east), following signs indicating "Cumberland."

6.0   Georgetown junction to Selleck. Keep left at the upcoming Y-inter-
        section; the other road leads to Cumberland. At 4.2 miles a T-
        intersection is reached: turn left (north) here and follow the roadway
        1.5 miles to the old Selleck post office and continue across the rail
        bed 0.4 miles to the old company town of Selleck (road's end).

        Selleck. Selleck was once the site of a large company town of
        five hundred people. Today perhaps a dozen families live on the
        site. The school and many company houses remain; outlines of
        streets, the hotel site, and house foundations provide tangible
        evidence of the earlier and large community. The big sawmill here
        was that of the Pacific States Lumber Company (300 M).

1.8   Selleck back to junction. At the T-junction continue straight ahead (south) on the highway to Cumberland and Enumclaw.

1.0   Junction to Kangley. Turn left on Kanaskat Road.

3.2   Kangley to Palmer, an old coal-mining town.

3.0   Palmer to Cumberland. The coal-mining ghost town of Bayne lies left of the roadway 2.2 miles south of Palmer.

6.4   Cumberland to State 410. Turn right (west) onto State 410 to Enumclaw.

0.8   Enumclaw city limits. Veer left at the Y-intersection, following State 410 to Buckley.

4.4   Enumclaw to Buckley, State 410.

4.5   Buckley to Wilkeson, State 165. On the southern edge of Buckley, turn off State 410 left onto State 165. Pass through the little coal-mining town of Burnett and on to Wilkeson, once a large mining town of nearly one thousand persons. At the southern end of Wilkeson keep to the right at a Y-intersection.

2.2   Wilkeson to Carbonado, State 165. Another old coal-mining town, Carbonado lies just to the right of the roadway (population 1,100 in 1920).

3.5   Carbonado to the Carbon River turnoff, State 165. Follow the narrow winding road along the Carbon River Gorge. About one-half mile beyond the bridge, State 165 bends to the right. Here, a paved road leads off to the left. Turn left off State 165 onto this road (Carbon River).

1.9   Carbon River turnoff to Fairfax. At exactly 1.9 miles, a gravel lane leads left down to the valley floor. The road is partially washed out and not recommended for two-wheel-drive vehicles. Park at the top and take the easy four-hundred-yard walk down to the Fairfax site.

Fairfax. The reasons for building a rail spur into this enclosed basin were linked to mining, not lumbering. In 1897, the Northern Pacific (N.P.) extended the spur from Carbonado up the gorge of the Carbon River to Fairfax, where the Western American Company engaged in the building of a town and a coal-mining operation. The mine officially opened in 1898 and by 1901 operated sixty coke ovens, the products of which moved almost entirely to Tacoma. Passing through three subsequent ownerships, the coal mine and coking operations closed in the late 1920s. What is important about the coal-mining enterprise is that it brought a railroad into virgin, up to that time inaccessible, timber. Immediately following the building of the railroad, the Manley-Moore Lumber Company in 1899 established operations at Fairfax.

Sawmilling at Fairfax, beginning in 1900 and terminating in the 1930s, corresponds well to the lumber boom in western Oregon and Washington. Employing 100 men in the mill (150 M) and up to 150 in logging, Manley-Moore daily shipped four to ten carloads of lumber out of Fairfax for nearly three decades. By World War I the sawmilling and logging operations had easily outstripped the importance of initiatory mining at Fairfax. In 1924, the Carbon River Shingle Company added a mill on the Manley-Moore pond, where it utilized the red cedar logged by the larger company. In 1932, the company shut down the big sawmill, the last industry on the site. Faltering under new ownership, the old sawmill sputtered again between 1934 and 1936, but in the late 1930s the sawmill was sold again and finally junked. Just as suddenly as it was born, Fairfax became a ghost.

The concurrent exploitation of mineral and forest actually brought about the formation of two company towns in the confined valley, both generally referred to as "Fairfax." However, Fairfax proper was the town of the mining and coking operation. Separated about one-quarter mile from Fairfax itself was the Manley-Moore Camp, a town of its own containing a store, school, doctor's office, hotel, and permanent residential structures. Although the mill town was larger, the mining town evidently was built more substantially. At Fairfax the foundation marks and old streets are clearly visible; at the sawmill town, only a few fallen-in and overgrown buildings indicate the town site.

One old photograph, a newspaper description (1962), and some remains on the town site supply the only available information

This Manley-Moore company house in Fairfax is no longer standing.

concerning the mill town of Fairfax. Because of the restricted space, the sawmill, kiln, and pond occupied most of the valley floor. Just north of the mill site there were a few rows of company houses (single-family) painted, as were the rest of the town buildings, green with white trim. Some concrete blocks (the only signs of the old sawmill), some scattered timbers, and the overgrown millpond comprise the site. On the western slope, just above the valley floor, stood the Moore home on a small eminence. Nearby were the bunkhouses, mess hall, barber shop, store, and twenty-six-room Manley-Moore Hotel of an earlier day.

12.1   Fairfax to Buckley. Return to Buckley by the same route (State
            165). At Buckley turn left (west) onto State 410 to Sumner and
            Tacoma.

13.0   Buckley to State 167 junction (near Sumner). Left at State 167.

2.5   Sumner to Puyallup, State 167.

8.5   Puyallup to Interstate 5 (Tacoma), State 167. End of trip.

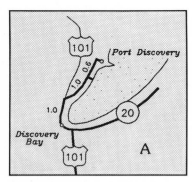

TRIP 2
214.7 Miles

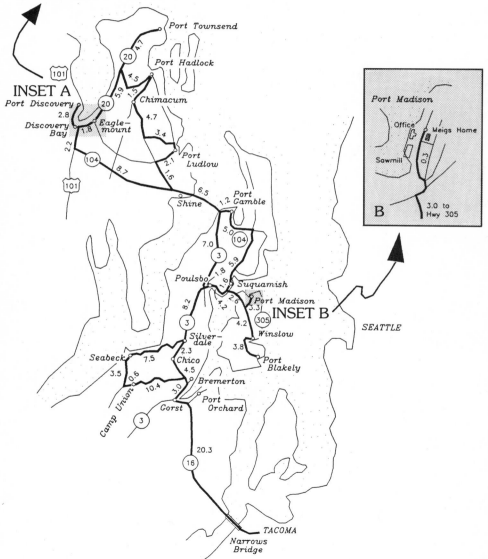

TRIP 2

PUGET SOUND LOOP
(214.7 MILES)

This loop from Tacoma encompasses eight of the sites of the great nineteenth-century steam mills on Puget Sound. Of all the big cargo mills that once dotted the Sound in the 1880s, only one remains—Port Gamble, which has been sawing logs for almost 140 years.

When these mill towns were founded, primarily in the 1850s, they comprised the only towns in Washington Territory and the only industrial base north of the Columbia River. Each of the mill towns typically had one "strong man," who, as part owner, manager, and superintendent, ran the town with an iron hand. Characteristically, the old lumber ports were founded by New Englanders, sea captains and millmen backed by San Francisco capital.

This long-gone era of sailing ships, rafting, and ox teams came to an end with the arrival of the railroads. By the end of the nineteenth century, the transcontinental lines were well established in Washington, along with many branch lines and logging spurs (see TRIP 1). The old cargo ports began folding soon after the building of inland railroad milling, and a nostalgic epoch drew to a close before World War I.

Itinerary

Miles	Place
Start	City of Tacoma, Washington. Follow State 16 westward from I-5. Begin mileage at the Narrows Bridge.
20.3	Narrows Bridge (Tacoma) to Gorst, State 16.
3.0	Gorst to Bremerton, State 3. Veer left at Y-intersection following State 3, marked to Hood Canal Bridge.

23

4.5   Bremerton to Chico, State 3.

2.3   Chico to Silverdale, State 3.

8.3   Silverdale to Poulsbo turnoff, State 3. State 3 turns left at the signal.
             Continue straight across the intersection as highway becomes State
             305 (east) to Poulsbo.

1.8   Poulsbo, State 305. You may wish to drive through the downtown
             of old Poulsbo, as the name suggests, a Scandinavian logging town
             of the nineteenth century. Proceed on the main street back up the
             hill to State 305. Turn right onto State 305.

4.2   Poulsbo to the junction to Suquamish, State 305. Continue on State
             305 (veering to right).

6.8   State 305 to Winslow. At the stoplight just before the Winslow ferry
             entrance, turn right onto Winslow Way, the main street of the town.

3.8   Winslow to Port Blakely. Follow Winslow Way to the west end of
             town and turn right (north) on Grow Avenue and stay on this street
             to the stop sign, 0.7 miles from the Winslow ferry entrance. Turn
             left (west) at the stop sign and follow the highway (W. Wyatt) around
             the end of the inlet and southward over the hill to Port Blakely.

             Port Blakely. Old-timers whose memories reach back seventy
             years or more remember Port Blakely as the greatest sawmill in
             the Pacific Northwest. Established on the north shore of a narrow
             inlet at the southern end of Bainbridge Island, Port Blakely was
             the most famous and largest of the Puget Sound lumber ports. The
             mill town displayed steady growth into the twentieth century with
             a notable spurt of growth in the 1880s. The town in 1881 included
             one hundred dwellings. In addition to the family units, the company
             town consisted of a hotel for 140 persons, a school, Masonic Hall,
             and store. Town population in 1881 hovered around 400 persons,
             the company alone employing 120 men in the mill and about 200
             in logging. Quickly rebuilt after the mill fire of 1888, the sawmill's
             capacity was expanded to 400 M per day. At the time this was one
             of the larger sawmills in the world, and company employment

Port Blakely 1970: a company home built in the nineteenth century.

was increased to twelve hundred men. During the first decade of this century, Port Blakely's population peaked at two thousand inhabitants. Thereafter, shipbuilding, long associated with the sawmill, began to eclipse lumber manufacturing at the site and, with the outbreak of World War I, the company leased out the remainder of the old sawmill. The 1920s saw the Port Blakely Mill Company close down the shipyards, abandon the town, and retire from manufacturing.

Similar to its contemporaries, the mill town of Port Blakely was an unplanned affair. At the upper end of the inlet stood the great mill, a long, narrow structure built on piling over the protected waters. Around the mill were dockage, booming grounds, catwalks, and an enormous pile of burning wood refuse, later encased in a steel burner. The town itself extended from the sawmill down the north shore toward the opening of the inlet and was constructed on two levels. Nearest the shoreline and on piling stood tool sheds, shops, and the company store in a cluster adjoining the east end of the mill area. On the second level, on a bank about ten feet above the water, a single line of dwellings reached eastward from the mill,

Port Blakely 1992: rotting piling and the mill skeleton.

beginning with the large T-shaped hotel. New units were added to the end of the string so that, by the 1890s, the line of houses reached nearly a quarter of a mile. The school was located on the hillside a few hundred feet behind the sawmill end of the string.

The site, beginning at 3 T Road, offers today only a few reminders of the past. Where the huge sawmill once stood, a concrete burner foundation and gutted mill, some bleached piling, and gravelly fill now silently betray a noisier past. The remaining four company mill-houses (10359, 10403, 10669, and 10671 Seaborn Avenue) have been substantially modified from the common original design, but at an earlier time they formed part of the coextensive string of uniformly patterned dwellings. Toward the opening of the inlet some recently built homes and summer cottages typify the suburban waterfront residential development (and impending development) tributary to Seattle, only a few miles directly across the Sound.

3.8   Port Blakely to Winslow. Return by the same route to Winslow. Turn left (north) onto State 305.

4.0   Winslow to the Port Madison turnoff, State 305. Turn right off State 305 to Port Madison and immediately veer left at the T-intersection after turning off 305.

3.3   From State 305 to Port Madison. After turning off State 305, follow the signs to Port Madison. Turn right at Phelps Road and at 3.0 miles turn left to Port Madison. The road then forks into three lanes—take the left lane (Euclid Avenue) another 0.3 miles to the old town core.

Port Madison. Little of modern Port Madison indicates its earlier sawmilling heyday. A dense, century-old second-growth forest stands on the ridge above the bay. Among the trees and down the hillside to the shoreline, contemporary homes closely pack the slope. On the cobble beach a little concrete is all that may be found. The only telltale signs of old Port Madison are a few houses of nineteenth-century vintage scattered along the shoreline and among the newer hillside residences. At Meigs and Euclid is the well-maintained Meigs home, which overlooked the shoreline mill office and sawmill.

The Meigs home in Port Madison in 1992. This beautifully kept house overlooks the historic mill site.

In the late 1850s, George Meigs purchased a sawmill at Appletree Cove and moved it across to Port Madison on the northern tip of Bainbridge Island. After the mill fire of 1864, the Port Madison Mills were rebuilt to a daily capacity of 80 M feet. For much of the remainder of the nineteenth century, Port Madison Mills produced about 100 M daily and supported a mill town of three to four hundred people.

3.3   Return to State 305 by route of entrance. At the highway turn right (north).

2.6   State 305 to Suquamish junction. After recrossing the bridge back to the Kitsap Peninsula, turn right on the road marked "Suquamish."

1.6   Junction to Suquamish, center of the Port Madison Indian Reservation. Continue on the main road north through Suquamish.

5.9   Suquamish to the junction with State 104. Follow the main road north from Suquamish until reaching State 104. Turn left (west) onto State 104, following signs indicating Hood Canal Bridge.

5.0   State 104 to Port Gamble.

Port Gamble. The 140-year history of sawmilling at Port Gamble, now a National Historic Site, makes this town the only surviving member of the nineteenth-century cargo milling complex on Puget Sound. Through all the uncertainties of changing technologies, markets, and timber ownership and depletion, Port Gamble carries on, and the fortunate visitor may glimpse the past of this well-restored cargo mill town.

Port Gamble was founded in 1853 by four State-of-Mainers led by Andrew Pope and Captain William Talbot, both of whom represented family traditions of sawmilling and shipbuilding in East Machias, Maine. For a mill site in the Puget Sound wilderness, Captain Talbot chose a rocky beach where Port Gamble Bay opened onto Hood Canal near the northern tip of Kitsap Peninsula. The location offered both proximity to the Straits of Juan de Fuca and a protected harbor for the sailing ships that would be carrying lumber for the next fifty years. From Maine came men, machinery, and white pine to build the first little sawmill and hastily constructed

An aerial view of Port Gamble from the 1960s. At the right edge of town is the Hotel Puget.

shacks of 1853. Shipping entirely to San Francisco in the early years, then gradually expanding with new equipment and building a permanent town, the four owners in 1862 incorporated the Puget Mill Company, the famous sawmilling empire of the 1870-1900 halcyon days of cargo exporting. Cyrus Walker, another Down-Easter who began as timekeeper in 1853, rose in position and power to become part owner and manager of the sawmills of the Puget Mill Company during the years of expansion. Austere, thrifty, and authoritarian, he enlarged the company control of timber, bought out nearby sawmills (Ludlow and Utsalady), expanded all sawmill capacities, enforced morality in the company's towns, and built for himself a baronial mansion of wood in Port Ludlow.

At a pinnacle of fame around the turn of this century, the Port Gamble sawmills were annually shipping about sixty million board feet of lumber to California and a worldwide market. Douglas fir sawed at Port Gamble reached Kimberley, South Africa; Shanghai; Tientsin; Bombay; Petropavlovsk; Hawaii; Callao; Guayaquil; and the Chilean ports of Arica, Iquique, and Valparaiso. London,

Sydney, Melbourne, and Tokyo could be added to the list. After
1900 the number and size of rail mills in the Northwest suddenly
increased, a condition that created soaring stumpage prices, intense
competition in lumber pricing, and a loosening of the hold of cargo
shippers on the California market, long the mainstay of tidewater
lumber production. The cargo mills that had not built up a large
foreign clientele failed to survive the new competition. Even the
Puget Mill Company began liquidation of its highly taxed timberland
during the crisis and, in 1925, finally sold out most of its holdings
(sawmills, timber, and towns) to Charles R. McCormick, Michigan
lumberman. The subsequent Depression made McCormick's move
a tragic mistake for, in 1938, the descendants of Pope, Talbot, and
Walker brought foreclosure suits against McCormick and regained
control of Port Gamble along with his intercoastal fleet, Oregon
timberlands, and sawmilling complex at Saint Helens on the Columbia River (see TRIP 5). Today Port Gamble is still an active company mill town under the ownership of a new company with old
names—Pope & Talbot, Incorporated.

Under continuous company control, the town of Port Gamble
is little changed from former days. Down to the smallest detail it is
a New England town transplanted right out of the previous century.
Certainly the crispness of tradition here reflects to a great degree
the early policies and desires of the company officials who owned
all the land and buildings. Reinforcing the New England identity
were millworkers, occupants of the town, many of whom were
family men recruited from East Machias, Bangor, or Boston.

Along the main street, which lies just above the mill and parallels
the bay, there are five principal buildings in addition to houses.
Restoration has provided informative signs and plaques to aid the
visitor. Near the mill gate and at the northern end of the street stand
the mill office and company store that provides the staple foods
and wares for Port Gamble families. In the past it carried perfumes,
lace, newspapers from East Machias and New York, and books—
all unusual items for company stores of the time. Alongside is the
mill manager's home, the Walker house, an impressive Victorian.
The Masonic lodge, which is located across the street, clearly ties
the town to New England not only by its presence but by its form.
With long, narrow windows and unadorned exterior, the building
rises two stories to a simply gabled and steeply pitched roof that
offers a sharp contrast to typically false-fronted little fraternal halls

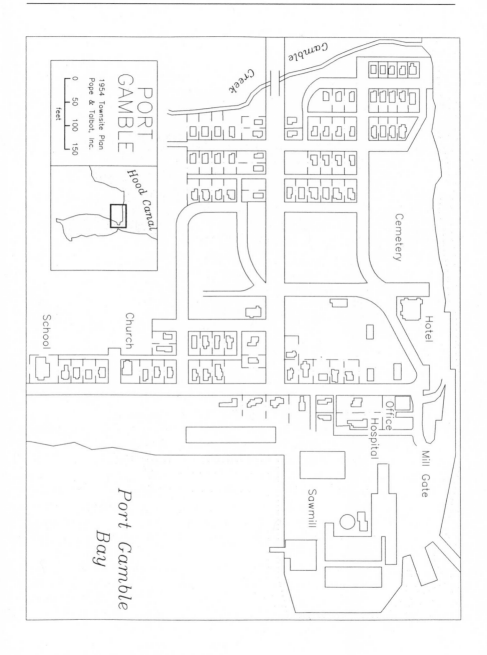

The 1954 town plat for Port Gamble.

One of Port Gamble's New England-like streets in 1992.

of Northwestern small towns. Toward the southern end of the main
street stands the Episcopal church, a product of construction in
1870, two years before the building of the lodge hall. The church
is well in keeping with the overall New England style with its needle-
point spire, tall neoclassical windows, and straight-backed pews par-
titioned by family and arranged by importance. The church
was, in fact, built from duplicate construction plans of the village
church in East Machias, Maine (1836). The other principal building
on the street, the community hall (later a union hall) was built in
1906 and conforms more to the prevalent area architectural style.
This was also true of the Puget Hotel (1903), which was razed in
the 1960s.

Many of the company houses, like the principal buildings, were
painted a gleaming white, but on restoration, a variety of subtle
shades were added. Neatly kept and simply constructed, the houses
are substantial two-story family units with gable to the street. Some
white picket fences and spacious, well-maintained lawns and gardens
around the houses add an atmosphere of overall neatness to the
town. The large houses near the office and store vary in style from

Port Gamble's Episcopal church, built in 1870.

elaborate Victorian to a simple but commodious two-story box frame capped by a hipped roof.

Other details in the town are distinctly of New England origin. The old elms and red maples that grace the streets were originally set out from slips brought around the Horn. In the geographical center of town there is a large two-block open space accommodating tennis courts and the outline of an old baseball diamond. This open "green" is surmounted by the cemetery, which occupies the top of a slight eminence, the highest point on the town site. Partially hidden by a profusion of planted elms and maples on the grounds, the cemetery lawns are rectangularly defined by a white picket fence. Even the smallest detail reflects the founders' desire to duplicate their faraway village environment: The tombstones are of granite shipped from Maine!

1.2   Port Gamble to Hood Canal Bridge, State 104.

6.5   East end of the bridge to Port Ludlow turnoff, State 104. Cross the bridge, and near Shine turn right off State 104 onto the road marked "Port Ludlow."

3.7   From State 104 to Port Ludlow. At 1.6 miles from State 104 there is a Y-intersection. Veer right here and continue 2.1 miles to Port Ludlow.

Port Ludlow. Port Ludlow is a major historic site in Washington. Here, in 1852, Captain William T. Sayward and his crew of Down-Easters began building the first steam-driven sawmill and first big mill town on Puget Sound. At its founding, Port Ludlow was the first major white settlement on Puget Sound and, for a brief time, the largest in Washington Territory. In 1858, Phinney and some

A photograph, taken about 1900, of the Phinney House in Port Ludlow.

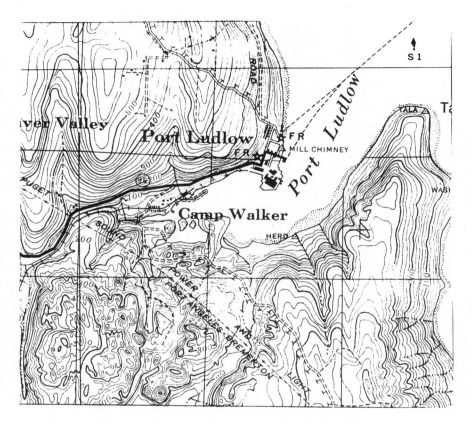

Port Ludlow, 1936.

associates from San Francisco purchased the steam mill and town and quickly expanded the daily production to some 35 M. Subsequently incorporated with the Puget Mill Company (Port Gamble and Utsalady), Port Ludlow became the administrative center of that great company. Here, alongside the Phinney Home, Cyrus Walker built the Admiralty, the famous wooden castle and showplace of the nineteenth century. From its renown of 1900, when the town boasted some seven hundred persons, Port Ludlow began backsliding. The Admiralty burned, population ebbed to five hundred in the 1920s, and toward the end of the Depression years the company's timber holdings in Jefferson County suffered a disastrous fire.

Port Ludlow circa 1890: the pond (bay), mill, and company store.

Thirty years ago the Port Ludlow site was a quiet ghost town. None of the original buildings remained standing, but the outlines of streets, foundations, and piling gave evidence of the town's earlier importance. Around the location of the long-ago-burned Admiralty flourished an exotic volunteer garden of trees and shrubs, a vestige of Walker's manicured garden collection gathered from around the world. Old ornate pillars and paneling of weatherworn white could be found in the tall grass around the town site. Below, on the beach to the south, stood the brick and concrete remains of the steam plant and circular burner stand. In a curious and restful way, sitting among the grasses one could almost return to the past, to sailing ships in the harbor, to noisy children in the streets, to mill whistles, the odor of smoke and freshly sawed wood.

A journey to the Port Ludlow site in 1992 is a shocking return to the present. The entire site has been bulldozer-scaped into a mass of curvilinear paved lanes along which front "condominium-style" buildings: moorage, beach club, conference center, tiered condos, and sales office. In the ribbonlike spaces between streets and asphaltic parking lots, some conifers create a bit of greenery. The

Port Ludlow in 1962: porch pillars on the original town site.

concrete burner stand forms the green rotunda at the park and marina grounds.

0.3   Port Ludlow to Chimacum junction. Follow the main road north out of Port Ludlow and turn left (northwest) at the sign indicating Chimacum.

3.1   From the junction to an intersection with the main road to Chimacum. Turn right (north) to Chimacum.

4.7   The village of Chimacum. Turn right at the crossroads and follow
           the signs to Port Hadlock.

1.5   Chimacum to Port Hadlock. At the crossroads in Port Hadlock, turn
           right and follow the road 0.2 miles, turn left at the Lower Hadlock
           Road sign, and drive another 0.2 miles down to the old waterfront.

           Port Hadlock. Port Hadlock was the site of the last big steam mill
           to be built in Puget Sound. Construction of the mill began in 1884,
           and Captain Hadlock sold the site in the following year to W. J.
           Adams, owner of the burnt-out Seabeck mill, who completed the
           Port Hadlock sawmill.
               Little information is available concerning Port Hadlock, but certain
           data may be inferred from census reports. In 1910 Hadlock precinct
           listed 463 persons, in 1920 only 200 persons. Therefore, it seems
           likely that the sawmill folded sometime in the decade of the 1910s.
           Further, with about 250 to 300 persons dependent on the mill,
           the capacity of the plant probably ran about 100 to 150 M per day.
               Some concrete portions of the mill structures, seaworn piling,
           and the skeleton of a town, including the company store–office,
           five mill houses, and a false-front store with boardwalks, exist today
           at the site.

4.5   Port Hadlock to State 20. Leave Port Hadlock by following up the
           hill and straight across (west) the main intersection. At a road inter-
           section 1.0 miles west of Port Hadlock, turn right (north); 3.5 miles
           farther on, the road merges with State 20. Follow State 20
           northward to Port Townsend.

4.7   To Port Townsend via State 20.

           Port Townsend. Port Townsend, a National Historic District, is a
           revitalized and well-known tourist attraction in Washington. Practi-
           cally the entire town dates from a construction period between 1889
           and 1893. The land speculation, lumber boom, and railroad aspira-
           tions ended in the panic of 1893, leaving a town built for twenty
           thousand persons with a population of only two thousand. Today,
           with seven thousand year-around residents, the primary industrial
           base is the large pulp and paper mill on the southern edge of town.

This store building in Port Hadlock is now a small café.

Prior to the boom of 1890, Port Townsend, the farthest point into Puget Sound that windjammers could reach under sail, was a seaman's town in addition to the logging and sawmilling that occurred there. The old steam mill on Point Hudson, built in 1881, was the only industry of the little seashore community during the decade before the boom. A few houses remain from this early era dominated by New Englanders and their architecture.

The boom produced the indelible Victorian character of Port Townsend. The overly large Jefferson County Courthouse and Marine Hospital are two great edifices reflecting the dreams of a century past. The massive two- and three-story brick-and-stone business district is a reminder of the same era, as are the picturesque houses on the bluff above the town.

10.6   Port Townsend to Eaglemount, State 20. Retrace the route southward out of Port Townsend on State 20. At the junction 4.7 miles south of town, keep to the right on State 20.

2.0   Eaglemount to U.S. 101, via State 20. At the junction, continue on U.S. 101 northward around the bay.

1.0   U.S. 101 junction to Gardiner Bay turnoff. Proceed through the roadside community of Discovery Bay. At 1 mile from the junction with U.S. 101, turn right off U.S. 101 on the Old Gardiner Mill Road leading down to the bay.

1.8   Old Gardiner Mill Road to Port Discovery. Follow the old highway to its dead end and a residence (Broders Road). This is the site of old Port Discovery. Inquire at the residence.

Port Discovery. The existing residence, although of more recent construction, sits on the original town site. Here, back from the low bluff above the bay, once lay the town core. The remainder of the town strung southward nearly two thousand feet along the shoreline and edging boardwalk. The small cobble spit below the bluff provided the site of the big Port Discovery mill, the only remaining evidence being the circular imprint of the burner stand.

South of the residence, 0.6 miles back on the road, is a modern restaurant and new condos. This location was the southernmost extension of Port Discovery—the end of the boardwalk and site of a large dance hall.

S. B. Mastick organized the Port Discovery Mill Company in 1858 and financed the building of the big steam mill. In the nineteenth century the sawmill produced about 100 M per day and supported a bustling population of three hundred persons.

2.8   Port Discovery back to the U.S. 101 junction with State 113. Return to the junction and turn right (south), staying on U.S. 101.

2.2   State 113 junction to State 104 junction, via U.S. 101. At the

Seabeck in 1992. About ten structures remain from the nineteenth-century mill town.

junction, follow the ramps to the left (east) onto State 104 and east-ward to the Hood Canal Bridge.

15.2   State 104 to the east end of the Hood Canal Bridge. Follow State 104 across the bridge and turn right (south) onto State 3 to Bremerton.

7.0   State 3 to Poulsbo exit. Continue southward on State 3.

8.2   Poulsbo exit to Newberry Hill Road exit, via State 3.

7.5   Newberry Hill Road to Seabeck. Follow the signs to Seabeck.

Seabeck. Here on Hood Canal in 1856–57, W. J. Adams and Marshall Blinn of San Francisco financed the building of one of the Northwest's great and early steam mills, formally the Washington Mill Company. As a lively sawmilling and ship-building community, Seabeck grew to a population of six hundred persons before the mill fire of 1886, which destroyed the town's economic base. Adams, rather than financing the rebuilding of the Seabeck mill, chose to move the operation to a mill under construction at Port Hadlock.

The old town site is basically a small moorage, an old general store on the waterside, and a state park and church conference grounds to the left of the present roadway. The office and hotel, nine old dwellings, and a school remain from the 1880s. All are located on the lawns of the conference grounds, the old residential core of Seabeck.

3.5   Seabeck to Bremerton turnoff. Continue south through Seabeck to a T-intersection marked "NW Holly Road" to the left. Turn left (east) here.

0.6   Bremerton turnoff to Camp Union, the site of an old logging town with a vacant company house to the right of the road and a modified store to the left.

10.4   Camp Union to State 3. Follow the main road eastward. Turn right onto Seabeck Highway to Bremerton.

3.7   Bremerton to Gorst, State 3. Follow signs to Tacoma.

21.8   Gorst to Narrows Bridge (Tacoma), via State 16. End of loop.

Inside an abandoned burner.

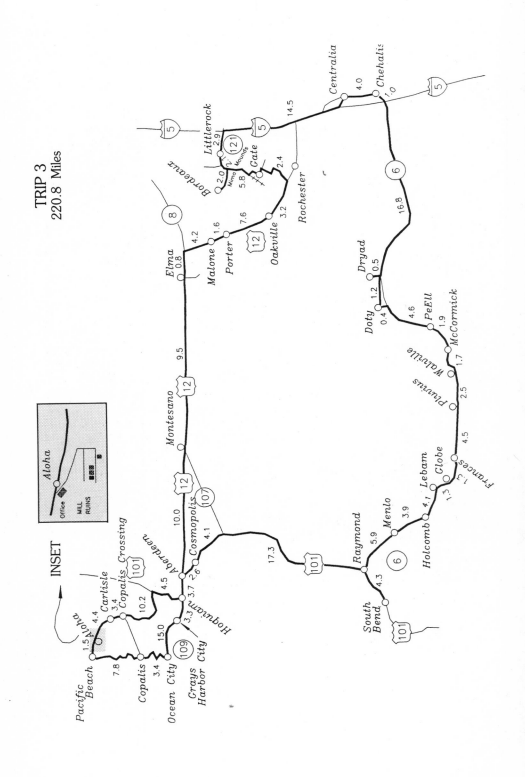

TRIP 3
220.8 Miles

INSET

Aloha

Office
MILL
RUINS

TRIP 3

WILLAPA HILLS LOOP
(220.8 MILES)

The Willapa country reaches back from the Pacific shore about fifty miles and lies between the Olympic Mountains and the Columbia River. Before 1880 this hill country probably supported the greatest stand of big conifers in the world. Individual Douglas firs (some around 380 feet high and 17 feet in diameter) rivaled the size of California redwoods, and forest density well exceeded one hundred thousand board feet per acre over most of the Willapa country. Around Grays Harbor some tracts were cruised at a staggering figure of five hundred thousand feet per acre. To speak of this forest today necessitates the use of the past tense —for by the 1950s, the old-growth forest had been cut out from the southern Olympics to the Columbia.

Long branch railroads to the Pacific coast, the Aberdeen and South Bend lines, were constructed from the main Northern Pacific transcontinental route in 1892. The railroads opened up this vast forest, and quick-to-follow sawmill boomtowns, founded between 1900 and 1920 by lake-states lumbermen, lined the new trackage, especially the South Bend branch. Big, clear-cutting, donkey-powered logging operations ("shows" in logging jargon) reached their apogee here in the 1920s. Retreating timberlines and the Depression finished off many of the region's ephemeral small sawmilling towns.

Itinerary

Miles	Place
Start	Chehalis, city of 6,500 persons and, with the sister city of Centralia, old center of railroad sawmilling in southern Washington. Note the oversize downtown area and abandoned mill sites along the railroad (west edge of town). Follow State Highway 6 west from town toward I-5.

45

1.0   Chehalis to Interstate 5. Continue across I-5 on State 6.

16.8   I-5 overpass to Dryad turnoff, via State 6. Proceed up the valley
             of the Chehalis River, an old lumbering region now in farms and
             hillside second-growth timber. Beyond Littell, an old sawmill town
             on the N.P. line, a roadside park contains a few remnants of old-
             growth Douglas fir. At 16.8 miles from I-5, turn off State 6 to the
             right (north) at an intersection onto a narrow paved road marked
             "Chandler Road."

0.5   State 6 to Leudinghaus Road. At one-half mile reach Leudinghaus
             Road, the site of Dryad to the northwest (left).

             Dryad. Someone with a feel for the classics and sense of the appro-
             priate named this "wood nymph" sawmill town founded in 1900.
             In 1892 the Northern Pacific built its South Bend branch (to Willapa
             Bay) across this level river terrace, the future site of Dryad. The N.P.
             line runs along the lower edge of the bluff on the north side of town.
             The existence of the town dates from the establishment of a sawmill

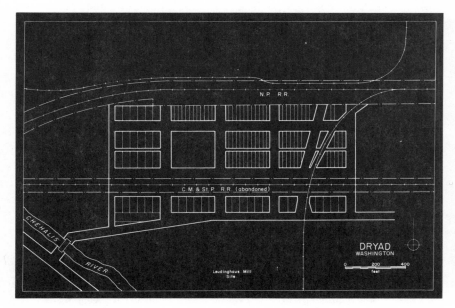

The Dryad town plat.

Dryad, 1963. This view is along the abandoned railroad right-of-way.

(135 M) by the Leudinghaus Lumber Company and the platting of the town site in the same year. In 1910 a second railroad line, the Milwaukee Road, drove its rails across the middle of the plat. By this time the town boasted a population of five hundred and for twenty years maintained a population of about 550. In 1930 the sawmill closed its doors, and the town's economy collapsed. First, the mill was razed. The Milwaukee Road then sold its line to the Weyerhaeuser Company, which used the line as a logging spur and subsequently pulled up the track. By the mid-1950s, even logging was on the downswing in the heavily cut-over backcountry. In the Western euphemism for failure, Dryad became just another town gone "belly up."

Dryad had a population of approximately fifty persons at this writing. Abandoned structures, houses fallen in, and foundations of others dot the vine- and brush-covered spaces of the town. The last vestige of commercial enterprise, the general store, closed in the 1960s. Because the store housed the post office, so ended, too, the official era of Dryad, the wood nymph.

A dilapidated house in Dryad, 1992. Few buildings persist here.

Loop through the town site to see the old mill site (between Leudinghaus Road and the river) and the church and school, both converted to residences. Closer inspection of overgrown space will reveal earlier home sites. Chandler Road, the entry road, lies on the east edge of the town site. The old Leudinghaus Bridge was replaced in 1972.

0.5   Return south on Chandler Road. Just after crossing the bridge and before reaching the highway, turn right on the road to Doty.

1.2   Chehalis bridge to Doty. Continue about one mile west along the straight country road to Doty.

Doty. As the extensive town site reveals, Doty was one of the larger mill towns along the old South Bend branch. The big sawmill (150 M) of the Doty Lumber and Shingle Company gave rise to the town in 1896. Adding grade and high schools, dance hall, and large community hall, Doty grew to over one thousand persons within the next twenty years and, in outward appearance, betrayed little of the company ownership that prevailed. The big company town and mill, however, went under in the 1930s, and by 1937 an observer reported that Doty had dwindled to "some families."

Inspection of the Doty site indicates that existing structures comprise only about one-third of the original town. A number of abandoned and overgrown house sites may be noted on the western and northern edges of the present town. The general store-post office, moved from across the street and renovated in 1919, replaced the original company store. Its walls contain a number of interesting photographs of the earlier town. The old mill site (north on river) was supplanted by a CCC camp in the late 1930s. Approximately twenty houses are currently occupied, primarily by logging families and retirees.

0.4   Return to State Highway 6. Drive south from Doty to the highway. At State 6 turn right (west) toward Pe Ell.

4.6   To Pe Ell, via State 6.

Pe Ell. Antedating the railroad, Pe Ell was settled sometime before 1890 as a small farm community, but the quiet agricultural life was short-lived. In 1892 came the N.P. line to South Bend, and with it, in 1894, the Yeoman Lumber Company mill (150 M) — the first of the string of large mills between Chehalis and South Bend.

Located in a farming area and midway on the rail line, Pe Ell prospered as a commercial center for logging camps and nearby mill towns along the tracks. In 1920 the school system registered 903 children representing 506 families, figures that indicate a population of no less than two thousand in Pe Ell and vicinity. In 1926 the Yeoman mill burned to the ground, and in the early 1930s the remaining source of town prosperity, the surrounding mill towns, collapsed one after another. By the 1930s the population had withered to less than one-half of its earlier size; by 1990 to 547.

Main Street, a paved portion of State 6, recently lined with vacant stores, particularly on the left (east) side of the street, has only three major buildings standing. Turn off Main at 6th, one block to the N.P. tracks and mill site across the rails. Along the loop back to the north one comes to a large but vacant residential area where deteriorating dwelling and foundation outlines mark the site of an earlier population.

1.9   Pe Ell to McCormick. Follow State 6 through Pe Ell and leave town
             by crossing the Chehalis River. Following State 6 southwestward,
             the valley continues to narrow amid heavy second-growth forest.
             Suddenly the valley widens to a width of about two hundred yards.
             This is the site of McCormick.

             McCormick. Founded in 1896 around the McCormick mill, the
             company town grew to a population of approximately seven
             hundred persons by 1910. The sawmill (180 M) roof and entrance

The company store and mill office in McCormick, 1963. The buildings in the background are no longer standing.

The mill office in McCormick in 1970. This building now houses a general store.

and mill office were ornamented with elaborate latticework, a touch of the Victorian in a hard industrial environment. The residential area included the land south of the railroad tracks (left of the roadway) and once held a line of prominent buildings extending down the hillside: the manager's home highest on the slope; below it the white church with its high, pointed steeple; and, two hundred feet below the church nearest the tracks, the long mill office. The remainder of the space between the tracks and hillside was filled with about forty to fifty unpainted bunkhouses, shacks, and single-family homes. In 1930 the large sawmill shut down operations, and by the time the census-taker arrived, only 140 persons could be mustered for the decennial head count.

McCormick is today a ghost town. All but one of the structures have been razed or have fallen in, including the sawmill complex north (right) of State 6. Of the town itself only the mill office, currently a general store, remains standing.

1.7   McCormick to Walville. Following the narrow valley, continue west on State 6 around an abrupt turn and across a bridge over a ravine. The Walville town site lies in the ravine about one hundred yards to the right (north) of the highway. A residence and abandoned buildings mark the site.

Walville. Taking its name from its founders, Michigan lumbermen Walworth and Neville, Walville began in 1898 and folded in 1930. The company town probably supported about two hundred persons and attained some fame for the large hex symbol of an arched black cat that adorned the mill gate. Utilizing Japanese millhands on the nightshift, the Walville mill counted seventy-four Japanese workers in 1909.

The sawmill was located at the base of the ravine along the railroad tracks. The town of shacks, bunkhouses, and mill office-store was sited across the tracks within the Y formed by Rock and Salmon creeks. The school and several houses once stood about two hundred yards west along the south side of the present highway.

2.5   Walville to Pluvius. Continue westward on State 6 toward the divide of the Chehalis and Willapa drainages. A small lane leads to a posted residence to the right of the roadway. The site of Pluvius lies beyond the N.P. trackage and left (west) of the creek.

Pluvius. Little is recorded about this appropriately named mill town. Census figures indicate Pluvius precinct (which included Walville) jumped from 251 persons in 1910 to 400 persons in 1920 and fell to 212 in 1930. By inference, Pluvius probably existed as a town between 1910 and the late 1920s and held a population of about two hundred persons. If this figure is correct, and assuming a majority of single mill workers, the sawmill likely produced some one hundred M daily. Nothing today remains standing, save a yard marker in the grass along the railroad.

4.9   Pluvius to Frances. Continue westward over the low divide along
           State 6 and enter the upper drainage of the Willapa River. About
           four miles after leaving Pluvius, the valley begins to open at the
           junction of Fern and Custer creeks. This is the old Habersetzer farm,
           the site of the Handy brothers Mill associated with Frances. The
           present town of Frances is located another mile beyond and adja-
           cent to State 6 along the railroad tracks.

           Frances. The Handy brothers started one of the earlier sawmills
           at Frances, platted and settled in the early 1890s. A decade later
           a mill fire destroyed the sawmill along with most of the small busi-
           ness district. In 1910, after substantial rebuilding, the town counted
           472 persons for the precinct census. By 1930 the population was
           about 250; today the population of the little village stands around
           50 persons. The old tavern and dance hall of earlier days were
           located left (south) of the highway in the large bowl-like depression
           against the hillside. Almost directly across the highway and along
           the tracks stood the linear town core: depot, store, and hotel. The
           prominent church, the last major structure not destroyed by fire,
           stands on the east end of town.

1.4   Frances to Globe. Continue westward along State 6. At 1.4 miles
           from Frances a large cattle shed appears in the field to the right
           of the roadway. The shed was built from salvage lumber of the
           nearby mill. A narrow dirt road leads over the tracks toward the
           hillside and mill site. (To enter the gate contact the owner, Dave
           Habersetzer, who lives 0.3 miles down the highway in the first mod-
           ern house on the left side of the roadway.)

           Globe. The sawmill town of Globe started up in 1898, and in 1922
           the Globe Lumber Company suspended operations and abandoned
           the site. Population around World War I stood in the vicinity of three
           hundred persons.

1.3   Globe to Lebam. Stay on State 6 to Lebam.

           Lebam. The town and the Lebam Mills and Timber Company take
           their names from a reverse spelling of one of the founders's small
           daughters. The big sawmill, the largest on the line (250 M), was
           built in 1900, and the town's population soared to eight hundred

persons by 1910 and stabilized until the fire of 1926 destroyed the big sawmill. Within four years the population had dropped to 413 and has continued to decline. The main town core, once located behind the sawmill, has shifted toward the highway. The old mill site, pond, housing (mostly razed), and a goodly number of saloons once were clustered north of the railroad below the string of houses on the low ridge.

4.1   Lebam to Holcomb, State 6.

3.9   Holcomb to Menlo, State 6.

5.9   Menlo to Raymond, State 6.

4.3   Raymond to South Bend. In Raymond, State 6 forms a junction with U.S. 101 (stoplight). Turn left (southwest) at the junction and follow U.S. 101 across the bridge and on to South Bend.

South Bend. In 1890, South Bend was a sleepy cargo mill town where sailing ships loaded lumber in the tidewater of the Willapa estuary. In the same year the census recorded 836 persons— three years later the town had swollen to 3,500 people! The reason for the boom was the exciting but unamorous combination of "three little words": *land, lumber,* and *locomotives.* South Bend had been selected as the terminus of the N.P. line from Chehalis to the sea.

The economic depression of the 1890s somewhat slowed the pace of South Bend, as did the platting and rise of Raymond just upriver, yet the city counted over three thousand population in the 1910 census. As it turned out, South Bend's future rested with events in the new town of Raymond: the faster Raymond grew, the faster South Bend lost population. Between 1910 and 1920 Raymond increased from 2,533 to 4,447 persons; South Bend dropped below 2,000 by 1920. In 1915 the new Milwaukee Road built its terminal at Raymond, already the *de facto* terminus of the N.P. branch. Between 1910 and 1920 Raymond increased its sawmilling capacity nearly fourfold to almost a billion board feet per year; South Bend's lumber production barely maintained 1900 levels.

South Bend slumped to a nadir in the mid-1950s, when population declined to almost 1,500 near the end of the decade (1,550

The Shone Building on Water Street in South Bend, 1963.

in 1990). The Lewis Mills (the old Simpson mill site at the north end of town) passed into the hands of the Willapa Harbor Mills in 1931 and closed down in 1940, leaving only the Raymond Lumber Company, which made up one-half of South Bend's payroll. In 1953 Raymond Lumber shut down and was dismantled for lack of logs.

Today South Bend is far from a ghost—employment in county government and shellfishing keeps the town alive—but the present is only a shadow of the past. The town is overbuilt, over-platted, and strongly stamped by building construction of around 1900. On the hill stands a symbol of the town's vibrant past, a majestic county courthouse worthy of a state capitol.

4.5   Return to Raymond via U.S. 101.

Raymond. This famous mill town is dominated by the idled Weyer-haeuser plant built on the sites of two earlier mills. The town, sited on a swampy estuary and built on piling and sawdust fill, is some-what smaller than earlier days, when it boasted eight large saw-mills, four shingle mills, and sixteen saloons. If time permits, turn off U.S. 101 into the downtown and drive along old First Avenue, once lined with false-front stores and saloons.

20.8   Raymond to Cosmopolis. Follow U.S. 101 northward to Grays Harbor. Large stands of second-growth hemlock, Douglas fir, and spruce, now undergoing a second logging, line this twenty-mile route.

Grays Harbor Area. As one enters Cosmopolis one also enters a continuously urbanized area simply known as Grays Harbor that includes three cities: Cosmopolis, Aberdeen, and Hoquiam. All three towns have lost population since the boom of the 1920s, when Grays Harbor was the world's largest lumber port and boasted the greatest single collection of big sawmills ever assembled in one small area. Hoquiam once supported six sawmills with daily capacities ranging from 150 M to 350 M; Aberdeen had eight mills cutting 140 M to 300 M; and the big Grays Harbor Commercial Company mills in Cosmopolis produced 300 M per day. Over eleven hun-dred loggers worked out of Hoquiam, the Polson Logging Com-pany alone employing eight hundred men in the woods. Similarly, twelve hundred loggers worked out of Aberdeen. Of this enormous lumbering complex only four mills remain: two in Hoquiam, one in Aberdeen, and another in South Aberdeen.

Repeated fires, economic troubles, and time have combined to erase much of the raucous character of old Grays Harbor. Aber-deen, once a roughhouse town of sailors, loggers, and millhands, and onetime center of saloons and whorehouses, has evolved into a rather quiet retailing and wood-products town. Most of the build-ings date from 1903, the last of Aberdeen's great city fires. Cos-mopolis also suffered a tragic fire in 1928 that destroyed the business district, forced closure of the mill, and threatened the town with abandonment for two decades. Cosmopolis revived only in 1956, when the Weyerhaeuser Corporation built its large pulp-paper plant on the old sawmill site. Hoquiam somehow escaped the all-too-common conflagrations and from the Depression years gradually changed into a stable industrial city based on pulp and paper and dominated by Rayonier, Inc. (now ITT), the inheritor of the once-powerful Polson and Bloedel-Donovan logging companies.

Worthwhile auto excursions may be carried out in the Grays Harbor towns, especially in the older industrial and waterfront sections. Hoquiam is the best-preserved of the towns, although the sawdust fill and plank streets are covered with a thin coat of asphalt paving.

2.7   Cosmopolis to Aberdeen, U.S. 101.

3.7   Aberdeen to Hoquiam, U.S. 101.

3.3   Hoquiam to Grays Harbor City. Follow U.S. 101 through downtown Hoquiam, and upon leaving the city turn left off U.S. 101 onto State 109, which leads westward along the north edge of the harbor. A long line of rotting piling stretches into the harbor. The landward base of the piling and the ravine behind is the site of Grays Harbor City.

Grays Harbor City. Touted as the future metropolis of Washington, Grays Harbor City was planned for the north shore of Grays Harbor about three miles west of Hoquiam. Eastern capitalists picked the site in March 1889 and formed a land company, the Gray's Harbor Co., to accomplish the task of planning and promotion. The actual town site was planned for a small ravine some one hundred yards in width where it opened onto the open expanse of the bay. At this location the main channel of the bay was separated from the town site by one mile of extremely shallow water, which at very low tide receded to expose the gray-brown alluvium deposited in this large eddy of the north bay. These tidelands, diked and dredged, were to be the future sawmill sites and the economic mainstay of Grays Harbor City.

Clearing of the town site began in the summer of 1888, along with the construction of a mile-long pier from the clearing across

Grays Harbor City in 1992. The long pier gives evidence of a hundred-year-old dream.

the mud flats to the main channel. In the middle of 1889 the first lots were sold (minimum five hundred dollars per lot) to the public, which stood in long lines during the night to ensure a good lot selection. A piece of promotional literature of 1890 described the town as "the only natural site for a large commercial town on the entire expanse of the Harbor" and assured the reader of forthcoming railroads, mentioning Grays Harbor as then containing thirty-five businesses. In 1890 one street, Broadway, was graded inland from the pier. Along the west side of the street were arrayed two hotels and a half-dozen false-front stores; on the east side, amid stumps and slash, were two small houses and a large false-front store. It is likely that this cluster of a dozen buildings represented maximum development.

The following year saw little change. The tidelands were still unimproved, except for the long pier, and the railroads and sawmills were yet to materialize. Later, the choice by the N.P. to follow the south shore of Harbor all but ended any hopes for Grays Harbor City, and the depression of 1893 sealed its fate. Today State 109, as it bends up from the bay shore, follows old Broadway through

Grays Harbor City in 1890. The long pier appears in the background.

the site, two houses and a little shingle mill. Across the tidelands stretches a long string of rotting piling, the only tangible evidence of the century-old boom.

15.0   Grays Harbor City to Ocean City, State 109.

11.2   Continue northward along the coast through Copalis to Pacific Beach. At Pacific Beach turn right from the coastal highway onto a paved highway leading inland.

1.5   **Aloha.** The sawmill burned in 1979, thus closing one of the last active company towns left in the Northwest. Aloha Lumber Company began production around 1910 and for seventy years produced about 100 M per day in addition to shingle production. Only four houses (two occupied, one vacant, and one dilapidated) remain of three long strings of row houses, unpainted except for the white trim because, as the story goes, the owners did not want attractive paint to increase taxes. The company store-mill office stands in front of the burnt-out mill and tall stack. The

Aloha in 1975. This aerial view was taken just before the sawmill burned; by this time some company houses had already been razed.

tavern across the highway and some scattered houses represent noncompany additions to the site.

4.4   Aloha to Carlisle. Continue inland and southeastward from Aloha following the paved county road.

Carlisle. Along the roadway are found remnants of a large company logging town. Seven line houses are a mere vestige of a string five hundred yards in length that housed about four hundred people in the 1920s. The company-style house is repeated in Onalaska (see TRIP 4) and dates town founding to around 1920. At the north end of the string, the vacant logging office adjoined the rail yards. Across the highway stands a concrete vault, the site of the bank. A vacant school marks the south end of Carlisle.

3.4   Carlisle to Copalis Crossing. Continue through the crossroads toward U.S. 101 and Hoquiam.

10.2   Copalis Crossing to U.S. 101. Turn right (south) and follow U.S. 101 to Hoquiam.

4.5   Hoquiam city center, U.S. 101 south.

3.7   Hoquiam to Aberdeen, U.S. 101.

10.0   Aberdeen to Montesano. At the east end of Aberdeen's downtown, turn off U.S. 101 onto four-lane State 12 across the Wishkah River and east toward Montesano. At ten miles Montesano lies to the left (north) of State 12; foundation marks of earlier sawmills along the railroad tracks speak to Montesano's earlier economic base.

9.5   Montesano to Elma, State 12. Stay on the main highway.

0.8   Elma to junction of State 8 (to Olympia) and State 12 (to Centralia). Turn right (south) on State 12, which follows the Chehalis Valley.

4.2   State 8 junction to Malone, via State 12.

Malone. This large company town (population around four hundred in 1920) was built by the Vance Lumber Company around the sawmill (125 M) along the N.P. line to Grays Harbor. The hipped-roof, box-shaped houses date the town to the 1910s period. The Black Hills rise behind the town site, and a long logging railroad once reached over the summit to connect Malone to Bordeaux on the east side of the forested upland.

Malone, inactive since the Depression, presents a sharp image of the dying company town. The store and post office and three solid homes of mill officials line the roadway, while four rows of little one-family houses, some still unpainted, and replete with house numbers, sit along the back streets of the town. Most of the houses are occupied, but others are abandoned. Pastureland and vacant lots once supported more rowhouses of similar style. The substantial concrete work of the mill site stands at the south end of the town above the large depression marking the millpond.

9.2   Malone to Oakville, State 12.

3.2   Oakville to Gate turnoff, State 12. A small highway sign indicates
          the turnoff to the left (north) toward Gate. Turn here.

2.4   Turnoff from State 12 to Gate. Follow the narrow road northward.
          After 1.7 miles, including right-angle curves, the road forms the
          stem of a T-intersection with an east-west road. Turn left (west)
          here and follow the road to Gate, marked only by a house (previous
          post office) and railroad tracks.

5.8   Gate to Bordeaux junction. At Gate, turn right before crossing the
          tracks and follow the paved road northward. Past the large Weyer-
          haeuser nursery, the road junction to Bordeaux cannot be missed,
          for it lies in the center of the Mima Mounds, an unmistakable geo-
          logic feature associated with glacial or periglacial events. Turn left
          (west) to Bordeaux at this junction.

2.0   Junction to Bordeaux town site. The road forks 1.5 miles from the
          junction. The right (north) fork leads to the old residential site; the
          left fork leads down to the sawmill and old commercial core. The
          upper town site is well marked by the large, dilapidated school-
          house on the slope to the right.

          Bordeaux. This company town rose in 1901 at the mill site of the
          Mumby Lumber and Shingle Company, both operations owned
          by Thomas Bordeaux. In the boom times between World War I and
          1930, Bordeaux included two hotels, a bank, and a number of
          saloons—in addition to a rather extensive hillside residential area.
          The population in these years stood between four hundred and
          five hundred persons.
              At this writing only four structures remain at the old Bordeaux
          site: 1) the large red schoolhouse used periodically for a barn; 2)
          the old Bordeaux home, which serves as a farmhouse and over-
          looks the town and mill sites; 3) a firehouse converted to a garage;
          and 4) on the lower slope near the lower roadway, two concrete
          vaults (bank and mill office), the only trace of the earlier business
          district. The outlines of a rough street grid, the town site on the
          lower slope below the house and school, is undergoing reshaping
          for an impending small development called "Bordeaux Estates."
          On the streamside of the lower road (left fork), in the overgrowth

willows and alder, jumbles of concrete, worn piling, and bridging mark the old mill site, which covered the valley floor.

2.0   Return to the junction at the Mima Mounds. Turn left (north) to Littlerock.

2.1   Road junction to Littlerock. Take road to right at the intersection about one mile ahead.

2.9   Littlerock to Interstate 5. In Littlerock, take State 121 eastward to the freeway.

13.5   I-5 to the Centralia turnoff. Take the freeway entrance marked I-5 South to Centralia–Portland.

1.5   Centralia exit to Centralia.

4.0   Centralia to Chehalis (old U.S. 99). End of loop.

One of two concrete bank vaults in the abandoned lower town site of Bordeaux.

The abandoned school in Bordeaux.

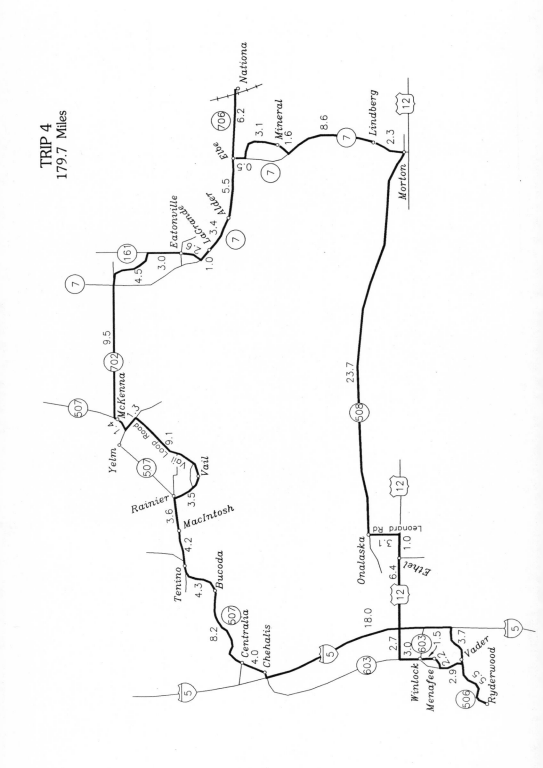

TRIP 4
179.7 Miles

TRIP 4

Nisqually-Cowlitz Loop

(179.7 miles)

This journey covers basically the lowlands between the Willapa Hills
and the Cascade Mountains of southwestern Washington. The boom hit here
shortly after the Northern Pacific transcontinental line reached Puget Sound
(1883) and the building of Tacoma commenced. Between 1890 and 1930
this area enjoyed prosperous times and a population higher than present
numbers. Where great old-growth Douglas fir forests once stood, today are
found farms, woodlots, and second-growth logging. Seven old company towns
lie along this loop, in addition to other old sawmill towns.

Itinerary

Miles   **Place**

Start   Centralia, city of twelve thousand persons, old sawmilling center,
               and locale of past I.W.W. union violence.

8.2   Centralia to Bucoda, State 507. Leave downtown Centralia by fol-
               lowing the main one-way couplet (Tower Street) northward out of
               town. After traveling through farmland and forested low hills, arrive
               at Bucoda, a village that lies to the right (southeast) of the high-
               way and across the N.P. tracks.

               Bucoda. Bucoda has had a long and varied past, rising with each
               boom and successively falling again. The lowland site was first
               settled in 1854 by Aaron Webster, who built a small water-powered
               sawmill on the Skookumchuck River. The Indians called the com-
               munity that grew up around the mill "Seatco," a name clinging to

67

Bucoda, 1992: little of the former business district is left.

the place until 1890. The new N.P. line to Tacoma in 1883 passed through the Seatco site and quickly produced a booming sawmill town. A Northwest magazine of the times, *The West Shore,* noted in 1890 that the town had a population of one thousand persons and the largest payroll between Portland and Tacoma. The major industrial concern, the Seatco Manufacturing Company, then employed 150 men in its sawmill and sash and door factory. At the time of the magazine report, the town, in addition to dwellings, contained five general stores, a meat market, furniture store, shoe store, blacksmith shop, and two barber shops, with a bank and hotel under construction.

In 1890, three men, Buckley, Coulter, and David, invested in the town and the development of newly discovered coal in the hills behind the town. Seatco then took on a new name, Bucoda, an acronym from the new investors. What the population was before the depression of 1893 no one can say with certainty, but the number must have been higher than the 855 recorded in 1910. Following the coal-mining boom, the new sawmill of the Mutual Lumber Company (200 M) brought Bucoda back to good times and

Bucoda, 1992: concrete remains of the mill.

a population around seven hundred or eight hundred in the late 1920s. The sawmill ran only periodically in the 1930s, and from the Depression years Bucoda has steadily declined in population, losing people at the rate of about fifty per decade.

The main street parallels the railway. At the north end stands the large hotel. At the south end stood the large sawmill, where a sign now commemorates the site. Follow the main street south to 11th and turn left, then zigzag to Seatco, Nenant, and Factory streets to reach the site.

4.3   Bucoda to Tenino, State 507. Tenino, too, is backsliding after earlier days of mining and lumbering. Note the elaborate "Tenino sandstone" buildings along the main street.

4.2   Tenino to MacIntosh, State 507. The site of MacIntosh lies alongside the highway on the east side of Clear Lake. Continue approximately 0.5 miles past a road (left) leading to the east shore of the lake. Look carefully for a small lane leading down the hillside to the MacIntosh site.

MacIntosh in 1970. Boards and piling are all that is left of the old town.

MacIntosh. The lakeshore was the site of the Brix Lumber Company sawmill (120 M) along the N.P. tracks. Built around 1900, MacIntosh persisted into the 1920s and supported a town of roughly two hundred persons living on both sides of the lake.

Nothing remains standing of the old town. The small lane leading off the highway probably represents the main street of MacIntosh, as indicated by a few weatherworn boards in the adjoining underbrush. Below the narrow "street" and across the N.P. tracks stood the sawmill, now but a lakeshore maze of rotting planks and piling.

3.6   MacIntosh to Rainier, State 507. Rainier was a major sawmilling
            town along both the N.P. and Milwaukee trunks. The town has
            undergone a typical decline-and-renewal over the last forty years. On
            the south end of town, just before entering Rainier proper, turn right
            off State 507 and take the paved county road (Vail Cutoff Road).

3.5   Rainier to Vail. Stay on the Vail Cutoff Road. A large water tower
            near the roadway signals the site of Vail. To the left, between the
            roadway and the two hundred yards to the Weyerhaeuser head-
            quarters buildings, was the town of Vail.

Vail, 1970: one of the few remaining houses on the former town site.

Vail. This large Weyerhaeuser company logging town was razed about twenty years ago. The slope toward the railroad yards and loading area was covered with houses until the late 1960s, when the company began tearing down and moving out houses. Today, only the streets are to be seen of a town that once boasted four hundred or more persons.

A close look at the houses and outbuildings in the vicinity reveals a gable-fronted, slightly hipped, rectangular, shake-sided house type scattered around the countryside. These are Vail houses sold and carted off from the town site; there is one in Rainier two blocks across the tracks.

9.1   Vail to Bald Hill Road. Follow the Vail Cutoff northward. At 4.1 miles from Vail at a crossroad, a large dairy farm appears to the right. Down the side road a short distance, the rows of white-painted cattle sheds are converted logging railroad-camp bunkhouses. Return and continue along Vail Cutoff Road. At Bald Hill Road turn left (northwest).

1.3   Bald Hill Road to State 507. Turn right onto State 507.

1.4   North to McKenna via State 507. Cross the Nisqually River and enter McKenna.

McKenna. Despite the failure of the mill in the 1930s, McKenna is probably the best-preserved lowland company town of the twentieth century. Built by the McKenna Lumber Company in 1908, the town featured unusually large two-story company houses with a midwestern flavor. The concrete hulk of the big sawmill (200 M) stands about seventy yards to the right (east) of the highway and north of the shallow depression that was the millpond.

The school is the only major structure no longer standing. The old company bunkhouse, some two hundred feet in length, has been converted to a nursing home. The company store is now a tavern. Most of the houses, although wooden structures and well weathered, continue to function as dwellings. On the north edge of the residential area are the better homes of the mill owner and mill officials.

9.5   McKenna to State 7 junction, via State 702. Immediately north

The concrete hulk of the once-great sawmill in McKenna.

of McKenna turn off State 507 onto State 702 and drive east to the junction with State 7.

7.5   Eatonville Cutoff to Eatonville. Cross State 7 at the junction and take the well-marked Eatonville Cutoff to the southeast. At the intersection with State 161 (4.5 miles) turn right (south) and follow State 161 into Eatonville.

Eatonville. Eatonville is not a ghost town, although the population sagged in the 1960s and 1970s and recovered by the 1980 census.

The Eatonville town plat.

Eatonville, 1970: the old millpond and idle mill.

T. C. Eaton platted the town site in 1888, and the town grew to become the most important sawmilling and logging center on the old Tacoma & Eastern Railway.

The most interesting part of the town lies south of the small-business district. Take Mashall Avenue (the primary north-south street) southward to Oak Street and turn left (east). Here, screened by Lombardy poplars, lies the old company mill town complete with an abandoned company store, mill office, owner's home (now a bed and breakfast), and row houses (most occupied). The idled sawmill, large conical burner, and weathered accessory buildings stand relatively unchanged. Within a short walking area, the site provides excellent subject matter for photography.

2.6 Eatonville to State 7. Continue southward from the Eatonville mill site (Mashell Avenue) and leave Eatonville via the bridge at the west end of the millpond. At 2.6 miles south of town, turn left (southeast) onto State 7.

1.0 State 7 to LaGrande.

3.4 LaGrande to Alder, State 7.

5.5 Alder to Elbe, an old but active logging town on State 7. Just east of Elbe, State 7 turns southward, crossing the Nisqually River. Do not turn. Continue on the north side of the river following State 706, the main route to Rainier National Park.

6.2 Elbe to National, via State 706. Some six miles from Elbe a logging railroad cuts diagonally across the roadway. To the right is a log storage area. About one hundred yards farther along the highway, turn right onto a narrow road that leads immediately to the site of National.

National. The abandoned company town of National once housed three hundred persons dependent on the large sawmill (200 M) of the Pacific National Lumber Company. In 1940 a writer for the Works Progress Administration described National as a town of small, red, boxlike cottages crowded onto crooked, planked streets and dominated by the large red sawmill.

Little described fifty years ago remains. Narrow lanes wind through a ground cover of thistles, vines, broom, and grasses. Here and there a remnant flower bed survives the weedy incursion. Portions of weatherworn picket fencing, boardwalks, piles of shingled roofs, siding, and boards lie under the thick cover of grass and brush. A little care must be taken around the site because old outhouse pits once pocked the residential area. Some scattered concrete blocks denote the site of the mill along the rail spur on the southern edge of the site. An occupied mill office–manager's home is the only standing structure.

Only a few broken reminders of the town of National exist today.

6.2   Return via State 706 to State 7 at Elbe. At the Nisqually River bridge (Elbe) turn left (south) onto State 7.

0.5   Elbe to Mineral Hill Road. After crossing the river, look for a narrow road marked "Mineral Hill Road." Turn left (east) here.

3.2   Mineral Hill Road to Mineral. Follow the winding road through old-growth stumps and second-growth alders, the latter branching across the road in places to form virtual tunnels of greenery in the spring and summer. Enter the north end of Mineral.

         Mineral. Around the turn of the century, Mineral Lake was a fashionable weekend recreational area sited deep in old-growth forest far up the Tacoma & Eastern Railway. The beautiful log-and-timber Mineral Lake Inn at the north end of town conjures up a time of straw hats, parasols, and long white dresses in the quiet lakeshore wilderness. Logging operations edging up the T. & E. Railway shortly ended the isolation of this idyllic lakeside retreat. By 1920 one big sawmill (100 M), five smaller mills, and radial

The mill office is the last structure left on the mill site in Mineral.

strings of logging camps had transformed Mineral into a boisterous lumber town of about one thousand persons. Although still an active town, the population has declined to about three hundred. The south shore park with a steam donkey on display covers the western part of the old mill site. One small building, a rail spur, bulkhead, and piling tell a quiet story of a much more extensive site. Back from the town on the south shore the regenerate forest hides earlier dwelling sites.

1.6   Mineral to State 7. Proceed southward through Mineral, following the main road. At the junction with State 7, turn left (south) on the highway.

8.6   State 7 to Lindberg. Brick row houses line the right side of the highway.

Lindberg. The company town of the Linco Log and Lumber Company grew up beside the sawmill (150 M) and the railroad that served the mill. The population in the 1920s reached a high point of approximately two hundred persons; by the 1930 census the population had dwindled to ninety-nine. Apparently, the mill and main portion of the town (store, hotel, and dwellings) were located left (east) of the highway and across the tracks.

2.3   Lindberg to Morton, State 7. Morton is the present center of logging in the upper Cowlitz River area and also the center of Appalachian mountaineers who migrated here from the Kentucky-West Virginia area between 1920 and 1940.

23.7   Morton to Onalaska. Turn right (west) onto State 508 in the center of Morton. The road skirts the Tilton River and carries through farm and cut-over country to Onalaska, which lies adjacent to the right (north) side of the highway.

Onalaska. Traveling north on the main street, old Carlisle Avenue, one encounters rows of lookalike houses, an abandoned theater and garage, a store, depot (now a hardware store and plumbing shop), church and parsonage, the Carlisle home, and a regional high school. A dozen or so other company houses and a Masonic Lodge hall lie off the main street. Of the mill to the west, only the

A circa-1930 aerial view of Onalaska. Many of the houses still exist.

tall stack, millpond, and scattered concrete stands remain. Truly, it is difficult to believe that Onalaska once counted about one thousand citizens housed in 175 single-family homes, forty small bunkhouses, and seven long, dormitorylike bunkhouses.

The terminus of the Newaukum Valley Railway, a short, independently owned logging spur off the N.P. main line, provided the location for Onalaska. Here, in 1918, W. A. Carlisle, a Wisconsin lumberman, built a vast sawmilling complex (300 M) and founded the Carlisle-Pennell Lumber Company town of Onalaska, presumably named for the old and famous lumber town in Wisconsin. Beset by diminishing log supplies, faltering national markets, and union organizers, Carlisle closed the mill during the Depression. Any hope for reopening the mill ended when the rusting hulk was scrapped for metal at the beginning of World War II. With the very reason for Onalaska destroyed, the town disintegrated rapidly to its present condition.

3.1   Onalaska to U.S. 12. Take Leonard Road (the southward continuation of Carlisle Avenue) across State 508 and drive south. Turn right (west) onto U.S. 12 at the next major junction.

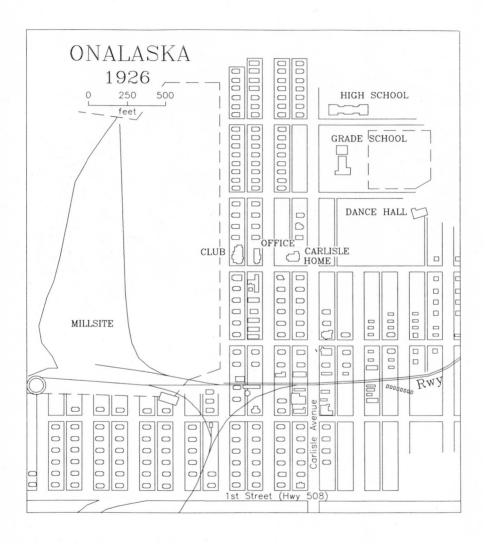

The 1926 Onalaska town plat.

Onalaska, 1992: the vacant Masonic hall.

1.0   Leonard Road junction to Ethel, via U.S. 12.

6.4   Ethel to I-5 overpass via U.S. 12. Continue westward from Ethel
           on U.S. 12 and continue across I-5 via the overpass.

2.7   I-5 overpass to State 603. Following the paved county road and
           continuing westward brings one to State 603. Turn left (south) onto
           State 603.

3.0   South to Winlock, State 603. The small farming town of Winlock
           has today a population of about one hundred but counted one thou-
           sand or more in the heydays of the early 1900s. The Winlock area
           is significant as the locality of the first big inland railroad sawmills
           in the Pacific Northwest. The original town site of Winlock was
           platted in 1875, but incorporation waited until 1883, coinciding
           with the year of Northern Pacific completion of the last transconti-
           nental link from Kalama to Tacoma. Four miles south of Winlock,
           the Ainslie Lumber Company's sawmill (100 M), store, and hotel
           operated from 1884 to 1893; about one and one-half miles south

of Winlock, L. B. Menefee constructed another mill (110 M) in 1889; in Winlock proper, J. A. Veness built a steam mill in 1892 and sold it in 1907, four years before it burned to the ground.

1.5   Winlock to Menefee. Follow First Street, the main street, directly southward from Winlock. At 1.5 miles the relic Menefee appears as an insignificant cluster of houses to the left of the roadway.

2.2   Menefee to the Winlock-Vader Road. Continue south past Menefee. This narrow road joins two miles farther on with the Winlock-Vader Road. At the Y-junction a search may be carried on for the old mill site of Ainslie, which would lie somewhere near the railroad (left) in this vicinity. Veer left (south) at the junction and follow the Winlock-Vader Road.

2.9   Winlock-Vader Road to the junction with State 506. At this T-intersection turn right (west) and remain on State 603 to Ryderwood.

5.5   State 603 to Ryderwood.

Ryderwood. Ryderwood, the past logging headquarters of the Long-Bell Company, must be considered the Northwest's most elaborate company logging town. Cougar flats, a narrow lowland in the Willapa Hills, furnished the site for the town, the construction of which began in 1923 following the building of the Longview, Portland & Northern Railway, a logging spur from the Columbia River sawmilling complex of Long-Bell. Laid out for forty-eight hundred occupants, Ryderwood included a school, church, post office, mercantile store, hotel, barbershop, hospital, café, and large community hall for meetings and recreation. Although the maximum population only reached about two thousand (with eleven hundred men on the logging payroll), the company built an impressive number of dwelling units: 250 permanent single-family houses; 75 skid-mounted four-man bunkhouses; and 2 large bunkhouses, each of which quartered about two hundred men.

In 1962, with old-growth timber cut out, the company placed the entire outdated railroad logging town up for bids. A real estate firm purchased Ryderwood with the idea of setting up a retirement village and attempted to sell or lease the substantial single-family houses to an elderly populace. The policy has been somewhat

There is still a boardwalk in front of the mercantile building in Ryderwood.

successful, and Ryderwood today is the home of some three hundred retired people.

A majority of the houses are still in good condition, although many have been removed, along with bunkhouses, school, and large hotel. The single-family houses are varied in style to suggest weakly a break in uniformity, which shows clearly along Madison and Monroe streets. The principal old company buildings fronting the wooden sidewalks of Main Street were once painted a uniform gunmetal gray. Around the intersection of Third and Jackson streets are several larger homes that once belonged to company logging officials. The Vandercook home on the southwest corner is particularly noteworthy in this regard.

7.3   Ryderwood to Vader. Return via State 603 to the junction with the Winlock-Vader Road (5.5 miles) and continue 1.8 miles on State 506 to Vader, an old and fast-declining logging town on the N.P. route. Note the stereotypical false-fronting.

3.7   Vader to Interstate 5. Continue on State 506 eastward from Vader crossing hill land. At the freeway turn left and take I-5 north to Chehalis.

18.0   I-5 to Chehalis turnoff.

1.0   Chehalis turnoff to Chehalis.

4.0   Chehalis to Centralia. End of loop.

Ryderwood, 1992: abandoned livery stable.

An old plank walk deteriorates outside the fire department building in Ryderwood.

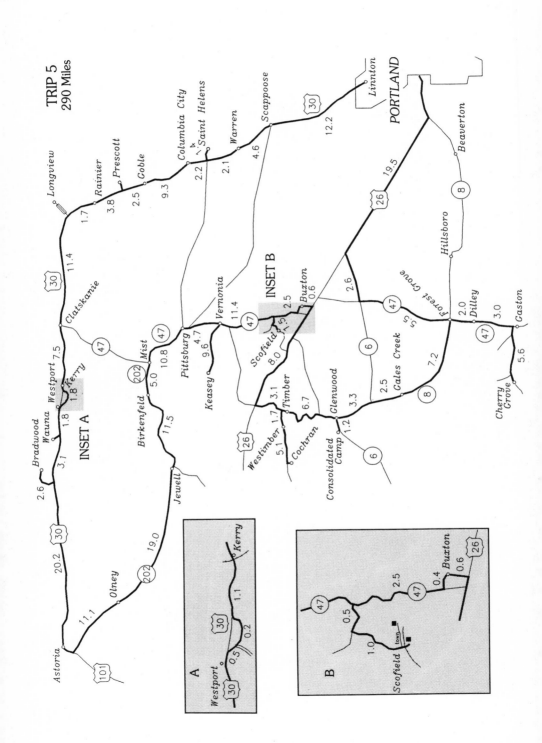

TRIP 5
290 Miles

TRIP 5

NEHALEM-COLUMBIA LOOP
(292.3 MILES)

Leaving Portland, the route winds across the Coast Range and cuts through the famous Nehalem logging country of northwestern Oregon. The return follows the Columbia River from its mouth back up to Portland. Plan on an overnight stay in the Astoria area.

The Nehalem country was opened in 1913 with the completion of a railroad (Southern Pacific) from Portland to Tillamook on the Pacific Coast. After World War I, the countryside of the Nehalem River Basin resounded to a din of felling axes, saws, and logging locomotives. Most of the trees were Douglas firs growing in large, even-age tracts about two hundred years old. Although not of great girth, the trees were very closely spaced, very tall, and characterized by straight, limbless boles. With stumpage volume running about one hundred thousand board feet per acre, the forest was ideally suited to then-prevalent clear-cutting railroad "shows." However, before the forested ranges were fully cut over, great fires beginning in 1933 raged through remaining old-growth. By the 1950s the great days of Nehalem lumbering were over. At this writing not a single major sawmill or logging operation is to be found in the Nehalem drainage basin.

The Columbia River portion of the loop follows a string of riverside mill towns dating back to 1856. Westport, Rainier, and Saint Helens are old cargo mill towns, the Columbia River counterpart of nineteenth-century Puget Sound (see TRIP 2). More mill towns were established along the river following the improvement of the railroad (S. P. & S.) to Astoria in 1907. Three of these newer mill towns were drab, isolated company towns of an older cast. Beginning in the 1950s, the great old sawmills on the Oregon side of the Columbia began to close. At this writing, their hulks razed, sometimes replaced by pulp mills, all the major Oregon sawmills are gone from the lower Columbia.

89

Itinerary

Miles   **Place**

Start   Portland, Oregon

19.5   Portland to State 6 junction, via U.S. 26. Take Jefferson Street
              west from downtown Portland. Begin mileage at the entrance to the
              West Hills tunnel, U.S. 26. Follow the Sunset Highway (U.S. 26)
              over the crest of the West Hills and westward through the
              suburbanized west Portland metropolitan area, around 1900 the
              scene of big lumbering operations now erased by farms and resi-
              dential development. Turn left (southwest) at the State 6 junction
              and proceed on State 6.

2.6   State 6 to junction with State 47. Turn left on State 47.

5.5   State 47 to Forest Grove. Continue south on State 47 through
              Forest Grove.

2.0   Forest Grove to Dilley. West of Dilley at Henry Hagg Lake is the
              active mill (1932) of Stimson Lumber Company Continue south
              on State 47.

3.0   Dilley to Cherry Grove junction, State 47. Just north of Gaston
              turn right (west) at the junction indicating "Cherry Grove."

5.6   From State 47 to Cherry Grove. At 0.4 miles after turning off State
              47, veer left at the Y-intersection and follow signs to Cherry Grove.

              Cherry Grove. Cherry Grove provides a view of a declining mill
              town a little over three decades after the mill closure. Earlier service
              such as stores, gasoline station, and taverns are now gone; the hill-
              side school is closed. Some houses have been torn down, others
              vacated. The hotel stood at 55234 Cherry Grove Drive with five
              business buildings westward from the hotel site. Only the concrete
              sidewalk gives evidence of the main street. The old mill site, pond,
              and foundation stand upstream from the town site (see Mr. Blair,
              55260 Cherry Grove Drive, for entrance).
                  In the late 1920s August Lovegren, the founder of Preston,
              Washington, built a modern electric sawmill at Cherry Grove, then

a small farming and logging settlement on the upper Tualatin River. The late 1920s proved to be an inopportune time for investment, and the mill went under in the subsequent Depression. Reopened as the Koennecke Mill (200 M) during World War II and salvaging timber from the nearby Tillamook Burn, the sawmill and town boomed until the timber ran out in the late 1950s.

5.6   Cherry Grove back to State 47. Turn left (north) onto State 47.

5.0   Back to Forest Grove, State 47. In Forest Grove turn left (west) onto State 8.

7.2   Forest Grove to Gales Creek, State 8. The point of origin of the disastrous fire of 1933 is located in the foothills west of and visible from Gales Creek. A cable-ignited blaze started at a logging operation and spread into adjoining timber. Fanned by a dry east wind, the heavily timbered hills of the Coast Range literally exploded. Convective currents, generated by the fireball, sent clouds to forty thousand feet, generating their own lightning storms. Ashes from the great fire fell on ships almost one hundred miles out in the Pacific Ocean. The blackened aftermath of the Tillamook Burn of 1933 covered 240,000 acres of timberland—up to that time probably the greatest continuous private stand of virgin timber in the Pacific Northwest. During the twelve years following the initial burn, big fires twice roared through the same country and expanded the burn area to 335,000 acres. (Much of the area is now the second-growth Tillamook State Forest.)

2.5   Gales Creek to State 6 junction. Continue northwest (left) along State 6.

4.5   State 6 to Consolidated Camp. The remnants of a large logging camp stand to the right of the roadway 1.7 miles beyond the roadside community of Glenwood. Turn right (north) off State 6 at the sign for the Oregon Electric Railroad Museum. Enter the site after half a mile on graveled road.

          Consolidated Timber Company Camp. During the late 1930s, after the Tillamook Burn, several large logging companies consolidated their efforts in order to quickly log the blackened but sound standing timber. The result of consolidation produced the last great railroad "show" in the Northwest. Subsequent burns in 1939 and 1945 destroyed most of the lines and trestling that once cobwebbed the ridges and valleys up Gales Creek and over the summit into the Wilson River drainage.

Today a few houses remain at "Glenwood Camp" along with a cluster of bunkhouses, shower building (in the original company yellow), and small outbuildings. The museum building is the old logging headquarters. The alder-covered space between the office and the highway once held the Glenwood Mill. By far the most impressive structure is the locomotive barn, along with shops and associated switching yards for the logging railroads. The old rail facilities now house a private museum and storage for relict street-cars and interurbans from Portland's past.

1.7   Consolidated Camp to Timber turnoff, State 6. Leave the camp back 0.5 miles to the highway and turn *left* on State 6 returning back toward Glenwood. At 1.2 miles turn left on the paved road to Timber.

6.8   Glenwood to Timber. A winding road over the divide into the drainage basin of the Nehalem River.

Timber. The hillside town of Timber functioned as a log depot and headquarters for the Sunset Logging Company of C. H. Wheeler (see TRIP 6). The big logging town flourished in the 1920s, when the population reached close to one thousand persons. Barely spared from the Tillamook Burn (1933), Timber had a brief revitalization with log salvage operations in the 1940s.

Timber today is close to total abandonment. A few company houses remain occupied, but other buildings, save a crossroads tavern, have been vacated.

1.7   Timber to Westimber. At the base of the hillside in Timber turn left (west) onto the road marked "Cochran." A flat area (with new home), pond, and bridge at 1.6 miles mark the site of the Westimber sawmill. Across the bridge and 0.1 mile farther on, three houses occupy the old town site itself.

Westimber. The small stream valley and surrounding slopes make up the old site of Westimber, a town established by the Eagle Lumber

Company in 1913 and home to about two hundred persons in the 1920s. The sawmill (150 M) shipped lumber out via the Southern Pacific railroad, which runs along the hillside just above the town site. The last lumber milled here was in 1935-36, under the name of the Nehalem River Lumber Company.

The town site today is marked only by an overgrown embankment (dam) for the millpond. Other, less apparent, signs of occupation comprise foundation outlines and piles of boards.

5.1   Westimber to Cochran. Drive westward along the gravel road past the site of an old CCC camp (0.6 miles) and continue on the main road to the right at the fork (2.0 miles). At the Coast Range summit of the S.P. line is the Cochran town site. Here the road forks in three directions; the center and left routes lead to the Cochran site, the immediate gentle slope of one hundred yards down to the tracks.

Cochran. Cochran, the rail summit, was a natural site for a big logging town, because loaded cars "had it downhill" in either direction.

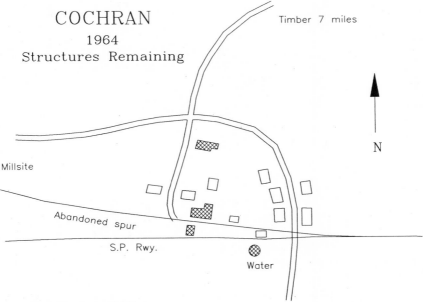

Structures in Cochran, 1964.

Cochran, 1962: house and old plank walk.

From its founding in 1917 into the 1920s, about one thousand men
worked out of Cochran. Before a fire destroyed much of the town
in 1932, there were two hundred persons living in Cochran itself.
The following year (1933), the Tillamook Burn seared the town
site. Two vacant buildings on the site survived until 1965; in 1990
no buildings remained standing.

Where the road crosses the tracks once stood the depot, of which
only the grass-mounded concrete stand appears. Behind the depot
along the road was the site of the town saloon. Elsewhere, ferns
and brush hide the old house sites and discarded stoves, bedsprings,

and kitchen objects. Large concrete blocks and pad give evidence of the sawmill (100 M) site, which stretches along the millpond to the west of the town site.

6.8   Cochran to Timber. Retrace the route back to Timber. At Timber turn left (north) on the road to Vernonia.

3.1   Timber to U.S. 26. Turn right (east) onto U.S. 26.

8.0   U.S. 26 to Buxton Junction. Proceed eastward on U.S. 26 over the summit (tunneled) and down to the junction with State 47; just beyond this major road junction is another road to the left (north) indicated by the sign "Buxton." Turn left here off U.S. 26.

         Buxton. All that remains of the business district is the large general store (now closed). Open lots along Main Street mark the sites of earlier false-front taverns and hotels. The remaining collection of houses represents about one-half the original residential area. Buxton in its heyday in the 1920s had seven small sawmills on its periphery and was a major logging town on the S.P.'s Tillamook line.

0.4   Buxton to State 47. Proceed to the northern edge of Buxton, turn left (west on Fisher Road), and wind down to the tracks and State 47. Turn right (north) onto State 47.

2.5   North to the Scofield turnoff, via State 47. A large and representative wooden trestle stands to the right of the roadway. Shortly after the railroad overpass of State 47 look carefully for a small sign marking a side road to the left. Turn left here to Scofield.

1.5   Turn off (State 47) to Scofield. After leaving State 47, a junction, Scofield Road, is reached (0.5 miles). Turn left here and proceed southward 1.0 miles to the S.P. tracks, the site of Scofield.

         Scofield. The town site and mill site lie across and south of the tracks, marked by the outlines of an old railroad siding. The siding marker is affixed to the barn of a farmhouse standing across the tracks (south). The old mill (120 M) of the Standard Box & Lumber Company probably stood to the east of the farmhouse, the front

half of which suggests the older style of a mill office. South and
east of the farmhouse is the outline of a millpond. Continuing south
on the gravel road about one thousand feet, one encounters the
remnant cluster of the old residential area and town site.

1.5   Scofield back to State 47. Retrace the route back to State 47. Turn
           left and head north on State 47.

11.4   Scofield turnoff to Vernonia, State 47.

           Vernonia. The town's buildings reflect the construction period of
           the 1920s. For some thirty years prior to the arrival of the railroad,
           Vernonia was a small village of some seventy to eighty people; in
           1920 the census recorded 140 persons. Within three years the town
           population soared to nearly two thousand. In September 1922,
           the rail spur was completed from the Tillamook Line to Vernonia
           and, with this link, construction began on the big Oregon-American
           Lumber Corporation sawmill (250 M), the largest in the Nehalem
           country.
              The Oregon-American mill survived both the Tillamook Burn and
           concurrent Depression years, but the old-growth timber was fast dis-
           appearing. In 1953 the mill owners sold out to the Long-Bell Com-
           pany of Longview, Washington; International Paper took over
           Long-Bell in 1957 and closed the Vernonia mill in 1960, the same
           year in which the great mill structures were burned as part of a
           movie scene.
              A leisurely tour around the town illustrates the impact of mill
           closure on a townscape. Population fell to about fifty percent in
           1960, and, even with some recovery, now stands below its earlier
           size. The stamp of the 1920s endures in the architecture of the busi-
           ness section and residential districts, where empty lots and vacancy
           are noteworthy. On the northern edge of town was the old Oregon-
           American mill, a site still marked by concrete structures and millpond
           to the right (east) of the roadway. Here, too, were once some
           seventy company houses, of which a short string remains along the
           right side of the roadway and a small cluster to the left.

9.2   Vernonia to Keasey. Just north of Vernonia's small business district,
           look for a sign designating "Keasey" to the left (west). Turn here.
           Drive the narrow paved road to its end and continue about one mile
           on graveled road beyond the bridge where the paving ends.

Keasey. Keasey was the big railroad logging town for the Oregon-American mill in Vernonia. From this center, which included a large roundhouse, the jerry-built logging railroads radiated into surrounding Nehalem timberlands. In the era of railroad logging (the 1920s and 1930s) Keasey probably had a population around six hundred persons, primarily single lumberjacks.

No town remains; four skid-mounted bunkhouses, one of them once the Keasey post office, stand at the Williams farm, the Keasey site. Under the thick stand of alders to the right of the road were the extensive railroad yards.

9.2   Keasey to Vernonia. Return by the same route. At State 47 in Vernonia turn left (north).

4.7   Vernonia to Pittsburg, State 47. Begin a sixty-five-mile journey down the Nehalem and over to Astoria. The route once was laced with logging railroads that reached out to the heavily timbered hill country of northwestern Oregon. Many small logging settlements and houses stand abandoned along the route, the entire length of which meanders through second-growth forests, some as old as one hundred years near Astoria.

10.8   Pittsburg to Mist, State 47. At Mist, another dying logging town, State 47 bends northward to the Columbia River. At Mist, veer left off State 47 and continue westward on State 202.

5.0   Mist to Birkenfeld, State 202.

Birkenfeld. In the 1920s, Birkenfeld was a large logging town and terminus of the Kerry Line, a famous logging railroad that wound over the ridges from the Columbia River to the Nehalem Valley. Birkenfeld is today but a roadside place—a store, a schoolhouse converted to a church, and a few dwellings.

11.5   Birkenfeld to Jewell. State 202. Jewell is just another logging town that has ebbed now to a few families. The old schools and residential area were located south of the intersection about 0.1 miles.

19.0   Jewell to Olney, State 202. Old second-growth forest along the roadway.

An abandoned house near the old school site in Jewell, 1970.

11.1   Olney to Astoria, State 202 and U.S. 101.

20.2   Astoria to Bradwood turnoff, U.S. 30. Go through Astoria eastward
            on U.S. 30 along the Columbia River. At 20.2 miles from Astoria
            (city center), a sign indicates Bradwood to the left (north). Turn
            left here off U.S. 30.

2.6   From U.S. 30 to Bradwood. Wind down the paved road to the
            base of the hillside, where, at 2.5 miles, the road forks. The road
            to the right (east fork) is the old Bradwood road, but it is gated

and posted. Proceed to the left 0.1 miles, where there is a place
to park near the railroad tracks. Walk the tracks back about six hundred yards to the razed town site.

Bradwood. Bradwood, built in 1931-34, is the last traditional-type
company town planned in the Northwest. Not unlike other company towns, the name of the settlement is derived from the mill
owners, Fred Bradley and Walter Woodard. The town site was
secured after a channel was dredged and the tailings used to fill
the cliffside swamp and slough. Completion of the mill and town
took place in 1934, at which time the sawmill began running two
shifts, each producing about 100 M.

Bradwood consisted basically of one long street of some one
thousand feet, given on both sides to small single-family row houses
uniformly constructed, spaced, and painted. Facing the planked
walkways lining each side of the street, yards were once tightly enclosed by white picket fences. Along the western end of the street
stood the mill office-company store and, beyond, the larger two-
story homes built for mill officials.

Of past times and lives, there are few artifacts: a few scraps of
wood, some household items in the dirt, and piling and boards near
the mill site. The bulldozers have prepared the site for its modern
occupants, a large metallic shed and a vacant modular house.

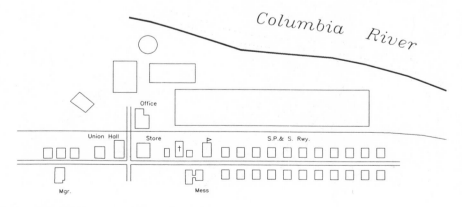

The Bradwood town plat in 1965.

2.6   Bradwood to U.S. 30. Return up the bluff to the main highway, noting the waterfall to the left of the roadway and the pump at the splash pool, perhaps the best evidence that Bradwood once existed. Turn left and continue eastward on U.S. 30.

3.1   Bradwood turnoff to Wauna, U.S. 30. Site of the Crown Zellerbach pulp and paper mill to the left of the roadway.

Wauna. Wauna was a big old company town, vintage 1914, which into the early 1960s lingered on as a ghost town complete with houses, hotel, office, recreation hall, and barber shop, all painted the company yellow with green trim. Crown Zellerbach, now James River, which bought the town site from Wauna Lumber Company, cleared the old company structures, except the water tower, and constructed a large pulp and paper plant on the old mill site and the riverside portion of the original town site. A layer below the pulp mill is the old sawmill site, a layer below the sawmill is the old Indian fishing village of Wauna.

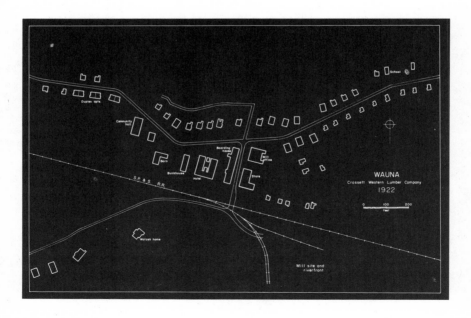

Wauna in 1922.

1.8   Wauna to Westport, U.S. 30.

Westport. For exactly a century the focus of Westport was the saw-mill that, through rebuilding and changing ownership, remained the economic mainstay of the community. John West in 1856 built a small water-powered mill and, using its first run of rough lumber, built the first house on the town site. Some ten years later, the water-power mill again provided lumber for its successor, an even larger structure housing a steam sawmill and rising two stories. In this am-bitious undertaking, West's son formed a company with three other men and entered in earnest the expanding cargo trade with Cali-fornia and ports of the Pacific Basin. Little is recorded of Westport during the next forty years beyond mention of a sawmill and town that in 1878 had a population of approximately 150 persons. The S.P. & S. Railroad completed a major line to Astoria in 1907 that ran along the hillside edge of the Westport site and opened a second possibility for lumber export. Unfortunately, a fire leveled the mill in 1908, but it set the stage for the entry of a wealthy lake states lumberman and for sawmilling on a scale theretofore unimaginable in the little town.

Myron Woodard purchased the burned-out mill site in 1910 and constructed a large electric sawmill replete with ten-foot band headsaw, new planer, and expanded loading docks. During World War I, the modern plant of the Westport Lumber Company ran three eight-hour shifts, probably cutting then about 150–200 M per shift. The mill town reached its zenith in the late 1920s, when the com-pany employed some four hundred workers and shipped lumber, with a specialty in long timbers, by rail and water. From this high point and a town population close to one thousand, Westport began to backslide. The short (1942–45) wartime upswing in lumber pro-duction all but eliminated the old-growth timber within economic reach of the mill. After one hundred years the last of the company owners, Shepard and Morse, closed and dismantled the Woodard mill in 1956, leaving behind 150 unemployed mill workers, a small town of three hundred persons, and a number of company-owned buildings: a grocery store, butcher shop, pool hall, seventy-room hotel, and thirty-four single-family dwellings.

Today Westport is a town of strong contrast between the old and the new. The modern pulp and paper plant just downstream at Wauna has stimulated new home construction on the hillside and a mobile home park near the highway in Westport. Across the tracks the old town core stands largely unchanged. A new fire station replaced the hotel, and the old business core is essentially abandoned. Most of the company houses near the center remain occupied (including the old West home, a bed and breakfast), but the row houses out toward the mill site have been razed. The mill site is a boat launch with the moss-encrusted heavy concrete work of the old mill nearby. At the ferry slip, the extensive and decaying piling of the cargo docks may be seen. John West's grave overlooks the town from the cemetery above the highway.

1.8   Westport to Kerry. Begin mileage at the crossroads in Westport. Travel east on U.S. 30 only 0.3 miles to a side road on the right. Turn right and immediately veer left onto the old U.S. 30 right-of-way. Farther on, 0.2 miles on the right, is an old tunnel famous for use by ox teams dragging logs to water's edge. Continue ahead on the old highway 0.2 miles to return to the main highway. Here turn right on U.S. 30 and proceed 1.1 miles, where a vestige of railroad trestle appears on the left side of the highway. This is Kerry.

           Kerry. Kerry in earlier days consisted only of a depot, post office, and store, but it was the jumping-off point for lumberjacks working over in the Nehalem country. From here the "Kerry Line" reached back to Birkenfeld, where the logs came "down the line" to be dumped into booming grounds, the sloughs north of the highway. An old house, once a rooming house, to the right of the road marks now the "town" of Kerry.

7.5   Kerry to Clatskanie, U.S. 30. Clatskanie was one of the larger logging towns along the Columbia. In the 1920s the population stood around twelve hundred persons, and some fifteen hundred loggers worked in the timber between Clatskanie and Mist. The current population of the town is about sixteen hundred.

11.4   Clatskanie to the Longview Bridge, U.S. 30. Do not cross the river; stay on U.S. 30 as it begins bending southward toward Portland.

1.7   Longview Bridge to Rainier, U.S. 30. Rainier is an old nineteenth century sawmilling and logging center on the Columbia. In 1889 the population numbered about two hundred people and, at the time, three log flumes converged on the town.

3.8   Rainier to Prescott turnoff, U.S. 30. Turn left (east) onto the road
           marked "Prescott."

0.5   U.S. 30 to Prescott. The tall cooling tower of the Trojan nuclear
           plant immediately upstream makes the Prescott site unmistakable.

           Prescott. Upon entering Prescott, one encounters a bewildering
           radiation of five lanes from a central roadway. The lane to the left
           (north) leads to the old mill site, now filled with dredge spoil from
           the river to create a county park. At the mill site, an occupied, moss-
           covered building represents the old mill office. Next to this building
           the hotel once stood.
              The town began with a sawmill dating from 1883 and, around the
           mill, a village known as Danby. In 1905 the Beaver Lumber Com-
           pany bought the site and commenced the construction of a larger
           sawmill. The mill machinery was ordered from Prescott Machine
           Company of Wisconsin and, so the story goes, one of the boards
           from the packing boxes was hung up along the tracks to denote the
           new town of "Prescott." By 1907 the sawmill (175 M) was in opera-
           tion along with a large company hotel. Following a destructive fire,
           the Clark-Wilson Lumber Company, the subsequent owners, sold
           in 1946 the town of Prescott, consisting then of thirty-three resi-
           dences, store, office, and cargo dock. The new owners were able
           to maintain lumber production only into the early 1950s.
              Wander about the roads of the town site. The many company
           houses are intact, a number are vacant; the pool hall near the hilltop
           is boarded up and dilapidated. Piling stretches along the beach.

0.5   Prescott back to U.S. 30. Return the one-half mile to the highway
           and turn left (south).

2.5   Prescott turnoff to Goble, U.S. 30. Goble was once a major log
           dump and booming grounds.

9.3   Goble to Columbia City, U.S. 30.

2.2   Columbia City to Saint Helens, U.S. 30. Saint Helens is really two
           towns: one near the highway and railroad, the other and older town
           by the waterfront. Turn left off U.S. 30 at the signal light and follow
           the main street toward the river.

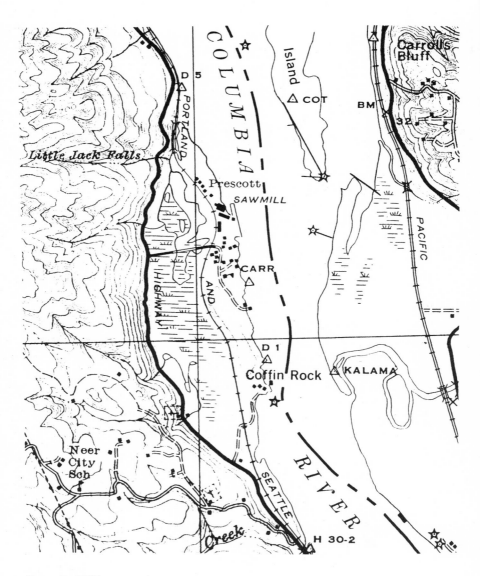

Prescott, 1936.

1.4   From U.S. 30 (signal) to old Saint Helens.

Saint Helens. The town site dates back to the donation land claim
of Captain H. M. Knighton, who built his home here in 1851 with
lumber shipped around the Horn from Bath, Maine (house at 155
South 4th Avenue). A steam sawmill, the Muckle Brothers Mill, was
built along the waterfront about 1880 but burned around 1890,
leaving only a little fishing and farming community of 258 persons
in 1900. In 1908 Charles R. McCormick of Michigan bought the
burned-out mill site for twenty thousand dollars, organized the Saint
Helens Mill Company, and completed in 1909 the construction of a
120 M capacity mill. By 1921 McCormick added three more sawmills
(under differently named companies), which boosted his Saint Helens
mill complex to a daily capacity of 460 M. Meanwhile, he had purchased the Masten logging railroad and started the McCormick
Steamship Company with six steam lumber schooners. The little
town of Saint Helens reacted to the boom by tripling its population
to 742 in 1910, tripling again to 2,000 in 1920, and almost doubling
to 4,000 in 1930.
   Saint Helens today is a town of three ages: 1) the waterfront cluster of nineteenth century dwellings; 2) veneered on the old cluster,
a second level of buildings (vintage 1910-1925), including the main
business area and reflecting the boom times; and 3) the last major
addition, the postwar construction near the highway and railroad.

1.4   Return to U.S. 30. Turn left (south) on U.S. 30.

2.6   Saint Helens to Warren, U.S. 30. Warren, too, was an old log dump
           and booming grounds of the 1920s.

4.6   Warren to Scappoose, U.S. 30. From Scappoose, a long logging
           railroad once reached inland to hook up with Vernonia and the
           big logging operations of the upper Nehalem.

12.2   Scappoose to Linnton, U.S. 30.

           Linnton. Within the city limits of Portland lies the district of Linnton,
           along the Willamette River near its confluence with the Columbia.
           At the turn of the century, Linnton was a mill town located about
           six miles downstream from the City of Portland. Two great sawmills

lined the waterfront of Linnton, each producing about 400 M per eight-hour shift: the West Oregon Lumber Company mill dating from 1901 and, just upstream, the Clark-Wilson Lumber Company mill of 1904. A note from a Portland newspaper, *The Oregonian,* in 1909 reported logs 105 feet long and 40 feet in circumference were being shipped from Linnton for use in the construction of the Ling Yen Temple in China. With a sawmilling payroll of one thousand men or more, the city of Linnton was truly a big mill town.

Both mills have been razed, leaving open land along the waterfront. Linnton, now a district of Portland, has stagnated as a periodized eighty-year-old town minus its earlier city services.

7.9   Linnton to downtown Portland, U.S. 30. End of loop.

Abandoned and deteriorating company housing.

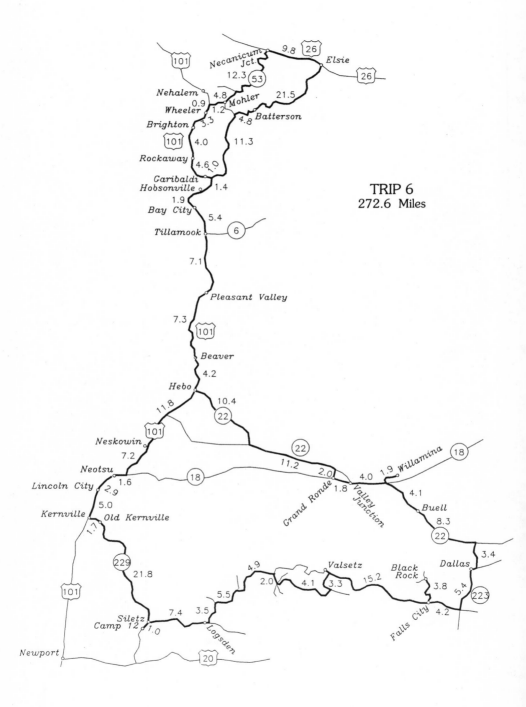

TRIP 6
272.6 Miles

TRIP 6

COAST AND SILETZ LOOP
(272.6 MILES)

The final route begins at Dallas, a sawmill town some fourteen miles west of Salem, Oregon (Interstate 5). The full loop back to Dallas connects two distinct lumbering concentrations: the coastal sawmill area between Tillamook and the Nehalem River; and the famous Siletz country between the Willamette Valley and the central Oregon coast.

The coastal areas once supported large old-growth Sitka spruce forests in which trees reached extraordinary sizes. Upland and interior forests blended gradually to become dominated by Douglas fir and western hemlock. The coastal spruce country experienced a major boom during World War I, when spruce was the principal wood used in airplane manufacture.

On the return to Dallas, the trip leads into the Coast Range and over rough logging roads up to Valsetz, an isolated outpost of a bygone era and, until its closure in 1984, the largest active company town in western Oregon and Washington.

Itinerary

Miles   **Place**

Start   Dallas, county seat and modern lumber town (population 9,400) dominated by one large sawmill (200 M) in the southeast corner of the town.

3.4   Dallas to State 22. From the city center of Dallas follow State 223, a one-way couplet, north. On the northern outskirts of Dallas turn left (north) off State 223 at the junction indicating "Valley Junction and Ocean Beaches." Shortly, State 22 is reached. Turn left (northwest) onto State 22.

8.3   Northwestward to Buell via State 22. Buell is an old railroad log-
             ging town and once supported a mill. Little of the old town is left,
             the crossroads store is closed and the school has been converted
             to a residence.

4.1   Buell to State 18 junction. At the junction (with a yellow flashing
             light) turn right and follow signs to Willamina.

             Willamina. Willamina, an old settlement (from the 1850s) and
             active lumber town, has a population of approximately seventeen
             hundred people, but the signs of decay are present. The sawmills
             that once lined the railroad have been razed, leaving a string of
             millponds on the south side of town. The one active mill, the
             Willamina Lumber Company (200 M), and the town's last mill, is
             located on the rail spur just west of the town center. The Conifer
             Plywood plant, by its nature heavily dependent on old-growth
             timber supply, stands empty on the east end of town and across
             from a town entry sign ironically proclaiming "Timberland USA."

Signs of vacancy in Willamina, 1992.

Today's population is slightly down from the 1980 count, and the small business district shows signs of vacancy and loss of services. Dilapidated and overgrown houses stand just one block from the town center. The newer residential areas (on the northeast) architecturally reflect a 1975 period when new construction stopped. Willamina is worth a close look, for what is seen there is a process repeated many times and in many places in western Oregon and Washington.

1.9   Retrace the road southwest and back to the State 18 junction. At the intersection turn right toward Valley Junction.

4.0   Willamina junction to Valley Junction, State 18.

1.8   Valley Junction to Grande Ronde, State 18.

Grande Ronde. A small logging center, rail terminus, and farm community until about 1940, Grande Ronde suddenly boomed during World War II and shortly thereafter. The wartime demand for wood and the need for immediate harvesting in the nearby

Grand Ronde, 1992: unpaved residential street.

Tillamook Burn largely explain the spurt that produced three 100 M sawmills along the railroad running through the center of town. Skid-mounted row houses were moved in to supply the rocketing housing demand. By the late 1950s, the timber salvage concluded, local private timber was clear-cut, and, national markets sagging, the mills began to fold and the town started to backslide.

Today the community is once again supported primarily by local farming and small-scale logging. The mill (Fort Hill Lumber) in nearby Valley Junction employs some commuting workers. A little string of auto-oriented businesses lines the highway. Turn right

The beautifully restored depot in Grande Ronde, 1970.

The old hotel, now vacant, in Grande Ronde.

(north) off State 18 at the general store. Note the overly large but well-maintained depot to the left. Cross the tracks to the remnants of a residential area in a grid of streets to the left of the road. At this writing some houses were vacant, some were in the process of removal, and earlier foundation sites could be noted. All that remains of the business district is the large hotel (now vacant) and the bank (now a community library). Continue north.

2.0   Grande Ronde to State 22. Follow the county road north from Grande Ronde to the old Grande Ronde Indian Agency (closed in 1925). At this highway junction turn left (west) onto State 22.

11.2   To Little Nestucca junction, via State 22. A winding drive through second-growth forest, valley farmland, and abandoned "stump ranches." Turn right (northwest) at the Y-junction and continue on State 22.

10.4   Little Nestucca junction to Hebo via State 22. Turn right (north) at Hebo onto U.S. 101.

4.2   Hebo to Beaver, U.S. 101. Beaver is a small logging town that
           once supported a sawmill, on the Nestucca River.

7.3   Beaver to Pleasant Valley, U.S. 101.

7.1   Pleasant Valley to Tillamook, U.S. 101. Tillamook has lost much
           of the sawmilling and logging flavor that characterized the city
           between 1910 and 1950. Old mill sites dot the slough and railroad
           (terminus of the Tillamook Line) in the northern and western part
           of town. If time permits, the county museum in the city center is
           well worth a visit.

5.4   Tillamook to Bay City, U.S. 101. Bay City in 1890 was described
           as a community consisting of a sawmill, hotel, two general stores,
           and about thirty homes.

1.9   Bay City to Hobsonville, U.S. 101.

           Hobsonville. Virtually all traces of the former mill town are gone
           today. Approaching from the south on U.S. 101, the site appears

Hobsonville in 1890. The long wharf collapsed seventy years ago.

Hobsonville, 1992: Piling and concrete from the nineteenth century.

as a low islandlike headland jutting out into the bay. The highway skirts this knoll, the backside of which has been evacuated for the roadway.

The fact that Hobsonville exists as a place is due to its brief life as a sawmill town. In 1883 the cobble beach around the headland sustained two small canneries and two or three crudely constructed houses, one of the latter being the port of entry for Tillamook Bay. The fall of 1883 witnessed the construction of a large steam sawmill, the Smith Mill, which surrounded nearly one-half the headland with a wooden coating of mill buildings, hotel, store, and dockage, all underpinned with piling. Local Indians and homesteaders furnished the initial labor and were paid in orders on the company store. When the sawmill was completed, the canneries were abandoned as the economic life of the community swung to the sawmill. Purchasing the mill in 1888, the Truckee Lumber Company expanded logging operations around the edge of the bay and up the Miami River. In 1889 the mill was daily producing about 75 M and probably supported 100 to 150 persons in the town. The panic of 1907 brought permanent closure and, thereafter, time quickly erased the signs of a twenty-five-year occupation. In 1922 the long wharf, which supported the larger buildings, collapsed, and by the early 1940s only two vacant and weatherworn structures remained on the site. At the present time, brush and alders hide a few scattered timbers, and bay waters wash concrete blocks and cobble-buried dockage along the beach.

The builders apparently followed no plan for the little mill town. Following the building of the mill, bunkhouses and hotel were constructed close by the docks. As the mill and logging operations grew, the slope above the mill was terraced to provide sites for jerry-built houses. The one and only road, paved with slab-wood and called "Sawdust Avenue," connected the hillside homes with the sawmill. Here at the Hobsonville site, a highway turnoff provides a historic signpost commemorating Captain Robert Gray, who discovered the bay. It is unfortunate that the historic marker neglects to mention the very town site upon which the marker is located.

1.4   Hobsonville to Miami Valley junction, U.S. 101. After the small bridge over the Miami River, turn right from U.S. 101 onto the county road up the Miami Valley.

11.3   Miami Valley to Foley Creek junction. The divide between the Miami River and Foley Creek (Nehalem drainage) is hardly perceptible and this delightful loop along the backside of coastal ridges follows a narrow lowland known for logging "big timber." On the hillsides, the second- and third-growth forests represent the chronology of logging in the area. In the lower valley of the Miami, the hillsides support stands nearly a century old; a logging era of ox teams and river drives that supported old Hobsonville. Roughly midway along the loop, the timber represents regrowth following the big logging operations of the 1920s.

At the Foley Creek junction, turn right at Foss Road. This is the Nehalem River Road that follows the old Tillamook Line upstream.

4.8   Foley Creek junction to Batterson, site of the large Hammond railroad logging town of the 1920s. Three company houses still stand to the left of the roadway.

16.2   Batterson to Spruce Run campground, Nehalem River Road. The road surface becomes gravel after two miles. Thereafter, partially asphaltic surface alternates with gravel. To the left across the Nehalem is the Tillamook Line, which crosses the river and leaves the valley at Salmonberry River (8.8 miles). Farther on, Spruce Run campground is the site of the Junker & Wicks logging camp, which operated from 1937 to 1945 and supported a school and about two hundred people.

5.3   Spruce Run campground to U.S. 26 at Elsie. Cross the Nehalem River, and two miles later reach U.S. 26 and turn left (west) into Elsie.

9.9   Elsie to Necanicum Junction, U.S. 26. Oney's restaurant in Elsie, a fixture since 1938, has a nice collection of old lumbering and forest photos. Two miles past Elsie is another roadside restaurant, the tourist-oriented so-called Camp 18, with an extensive outdoor collection of logging paraphernalia. At Necanicum Junction turn left (south) onto State 53.

18.3   Necanicum Junction to U.S. 101, via State 53. Follow the state highway southward, keeping to the left at the Y-junction about twelve miles down the road. Stay on State 53, crossing the Nehalem River just before Mohler and then on another mile to U.S. 101, where you turn left (south) to Wheeler.

0.9   State 53 junction to Wheeler via U.S. 101.

Wheeler. Wheeler is actually two towns, the old company town of Wheeler and the more recently incorporated town of Wheeler, the modern business district. About one-half mile south of present town center, the old company town is to be found. The Wheeler mill site lies across the tracks along the river estuary, where an extensive level area, rotting piling, and concrete stands give mute testimony to the once-great mill. The old residential mill town lies atop the low bluff east of the highway.

    C. H. Wheeler and John DuBois financed the construction of this sawmill and ran the company between 1913 and 1925. From 1925 until its closure in 1932, the big 200 M capacity plant operated under the name of the Westwood Lumber Company. The big logging operations of C. H. Wheeler were centered some thirty miles inland along the old Southern Pacific's Tillamook Line (see TRIP 5).

Wheeler's extensive mill site and piling.

3.3   Wheeler to Brighton, U.S. 101.

Brighton. The Brighton mill of the Watt Brothers opened in 1912 and closed in 1926. Fires seemed to plague the big rail sawmill (200 M) and ultimately forced its closure. In 1924, the town of Brighton burned to the ground. Undaunted, the company rebuilt the town and established a fine new logging camp at Rector (above Batterson). A forest fire in 1926 burned through much of the company's timber and destroyed Rector in the process. The Brighton mill never reopened.

The site arrangement is similar to Wheeler. A boat moorage stands on the site of the Brighton mill, and a few rotting pilings mark the old dockage. To the left (east) of the highway lies the hillside town site where a few of the old 1920s millhouses persist.

4.0   Brighton to Rockaway, U.S. 101.

4.6   Rockaway to Garibaldi, U.S. 101. Within a decade after the closure of nearby Hobsonville, the Whitney Lumber Company constructed

A hillside house above the abandoned Brighton mill site.

at Garibaldi the largest sawmill on Tillamook Bay (250 M). The Hammond-Tillamook Lumber Company bought the mill in the late 1920s. The old Hammond mill suffered through closure in 1935, a reopening in 1941-1946, a closure after the war, and partial activity as a plywood plant and sawmill until about 1970. Today, the tall stack and a few mill structures (commercialized) mark the east end of town. Drive up First or Second streets to get a taste of 1920s mill housing (occupied). Garibaldi, an active fishing port, tourist focus, and low-order retailing town, still looks as if it stepped right out of the 1920s (1990 population 850).

28.3   Garibaldi to Hebo. Retrace the route along U.S. 101 through Tillamook to Hebo. At Hebo veer right, staying on U.S. 101.

11.8   Hebo to Neskowin, U.S. 101.

7.2   Neskowin to State 18 junction, U.S. 101.

1.6   Junction 18 to Neotsu, via U.S. 101.

2.9   Neotsu to Lincoln City on U.S. 101.

5.0   Lincoln City to Kernville. Following U.S. 101, pass through several
             small coastal communities. Kernville is located at the U.S. 101
             bridge over the Siletz River. Turn left (east) off U.S. 101 onto State
             229 just before the bridge. Before turning, note old piling and con-
             crete to the right, remnants of the Kernville sawmill (100 M) on
             the Siletz River.

1.7   Kernville to Old Kernville, State 229.

             Kernville. The original site of Kernville lies on the floodplain of
             the Siletz River immediately adjoining the river bank. A mobile
             home–vacation home park currently occupies the level portion of
             the site.
                 From 1900 to 1925 Kernville was a booming log port from which
             log rafts, assembled along the Siletz, were tugged out to Siletz Bay
             and over the bar. The building of U.S. 101 and the bridging of
             the Siletz two miles downstream brought to Kernville a major reloca-
             tion that left the upstream site abandoned.

21.8   Old Kernville to Siletz, State 229. The winding road along the Siletz
             River offers a quiet journey through second-growth forest and small
             farms. Along the valley floor once stood one of the world's great
             Sitka spruce forests, with some tracts averaging 150,000 board feet
             per acre. Rotting stumps in fields and under second-growth cover
             attest to the size of the trees in the Siletz country. At one point (11.5
             miles), two large spruce trees, one forty-six feet in circumference,
             stand in a partially cleared field to the right of the roadway. The
             town of Siletz, one-time logging hub and linked to sawmilling in
             Toledo, has declined visibly from its former days.

1.0   Siletz to Camp 12, State 229.

             Camp Twelve. The present roadway cuts through Camp Twelve,
             a logging center twelve miles up the company railroad from the
             Johnson Mill in Toledo (now Georgia-Pacific), one of the great
             old (1917) mills of the Oregon Coast Range. With a capacity of
             400 M and initially specializing in spruce milling, the mill sup-
             ported a far-ranging railroad system in the Siletz drainage. The

Siletz Valley, 1992. This great spruce is evidence of the once extensive old-growth forest here.

Camp Twelve in 1992.

family community at Camp Twelve was based on that railroad system and located at the Y, where the line split into upstream and downstream branches.

The present community of Camp Twelve is comprised of eleven original family houses and a scattering of more recent homes. Five houses stand on line to the right of the road, where they once fronted the downstream rail line. Across the abandoned rail bed, south of the string, are sites of another housing string. Across the highway to the left (east) are some standing houses along what was the old main line and the upstream branch.

1.0   Return to Siletz, State 229. At the T-intersection in Siletz turn right (east) and proceed along the Siletz River to Logsden.

23.8   Logsden to Valsetz. Logsden, a small vestige of the earlier logging town, is a good place to check gas, water, and spare tire and to ask questions. The next forty miles carry over rough but passable logging roads to the upland site of abandoned Valsetz.

        Cross over the bridge (Siletz River) at Logsden and take the first road to the left (north) at the Logsden Community Club (on the site of the old Logsden schoolhouse). About 1.5 miles from the turnoff at Logsden, the remains of a logging camp (Upper Farm), a string of prefabricated houses, appears to the left of the roadway. At the junction to Moonshine Park (3.5 miles), take the gravel private road to the right. Keep on the gravel road to the northeast, following the valley of the Siletz lower gorge. Shortly after first crossing the river (7.5 miles), veer right and down at the Y-fork in the road and recross the river (9.8 miles). At 10.7 miles, cross Sunshine Creek. At 13.7 miles from Logsden, a T-intersection is reached. Turn right (south) here, passing the long-abandoned site of Camp Russell. About two miles farther on, roads branch in four directions: take the primary road (second from left). At twenty miles from Logsden, turn left at another T-intersection and wind over the hills to the northwest. At the Valsetz entrance, turn left at yet another T-intersection at 23.3 miles from Logsden. The road, once gated and posted at the Valsetz entrance, is now open to the public. A half-mile drive along a paved road brings you to the center of the town site.

Valsetz. Valsetz is a town in past tense. It lasted seventy-five years until Boise-Cascade's fateful decision to close the mill and raze the town in 1984. The mill was dismantled and burned, the company houses were wrecked with company logging machinery, and the site was plowed and planted in Douglas fir seedlings. The town's remaining residents moved "over the hill," down to the Willamette Valley, and dispersed in lowland communities. The site today shows only the paved road (old Cadillac Avenue) and outlines of streets at right angles. Surviving daffodils bespeak a time of picket fences, front yards, and board walkways.

Valsetz was an outgrowth of successive jumps in cutting from the Willamette Valley carried out by the Cobbs & Mitchell Company. The initial operations of the company focused at Falls City (around 1900–1910) on the valley periphery and, later, logging expanded westward across the Coast Range summit, reaching the Siletz basin just before 1920. In 1919 the Valley & Siletz Railroad, with ninety-one percent of stock held by Cobbs & Mitchell, pushed over the twelve-hundred-foot summit and dropped one hundred feet into a small valley on South Fork of the Siletz River. Three years after founding the company logging town of Valsetz, a large sawmill (200 M) was added.

Valsetz, 1939.

The population of Valsetz in the 1920s stood around three hundred mostly single men, but over the next twenty years the town's population doubled and, despite mill closure during the early 1930s, logging subsequently expanded along with sawmilling production (three shifts). The sustained growth of Valsetz was accompanied by a shift toward married mill workers and loggers and housing for them. In 1947, when H. A. Templeton purchased the town, mill, and railroad stock and formed the Valsetz Lumber Company, the town of Valsetz (population 750) consisted of 160 company houses, about 30 four-man bunkhouses, a store, garages, and a school. Ominously, of the 29,700 acres of timberland involved in the transaction, about 20,000 acres had been cut over during the previous twenty-seven years. Valsetz peaked in size in the early 1950s, when 260 men were employed in the mill, 125 in logging operations, and about 1,100 people resided in the town (1954). The sawmill was converted to plywood production in 1957, just two years before Templeton sold out to the Boise-Cascade Corporation. With operations cut back to plywood production and the use of logging trucks to reach the last old-growth parcels, the railroad was dismantled in 1978. The sudden closure, destruction, and scorched-earth policy in 1984 caused much ill feeling toward Boise-Cascade, whose tree-like logo was referred to as the "barbed shaft."

The striking feature about Valsetz, apart from its isolated and anachronistic persistence, was the simplicity of the ground plan (see map, page 124). Main Street, with its church, store-recreation hall, superintendent's home, mill office, and guest house was the focus of the town. At a right angle to Main, Cadillac Avenue—named by the Michigan founders—stretched over one-half mile and formed the residential core of cottages. Now all gone, the town is a true ghost. Pause on this tree-covered grave. Perhaps you may hear the mill whistle, the squeals of children walking along Cadillac to school, or smell the burning wood residue, the cooking of evening meals, or view dimly the big mill, the row houses and planked walks.

15.2   Valsetz to Falls City. Follow the main road eastward out of the Valsetz site, go straight ahead at the T-intersection, and continue on the two-lane gravel road over "The Hill" to the Willamette Valley. Paved road is encountered shortly before Falls City.

3.8   Falls City to Black Rock. Immediately after crossing the bridge into the center of Falls City, turn left (northwest) and follow the paved road that shortly gives way to graveled surface. At 3.8 miles from Falls City, the valley opens on both sides of the road. This is the site of Black Rock.

Black Rock. The business core was located to the right of the road. Where an empty mobile home stands now, the town saloon once

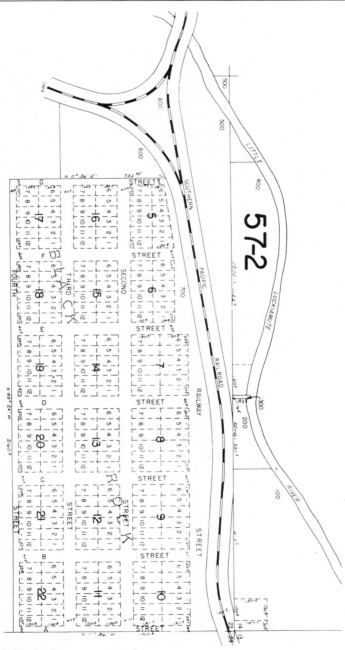

The Black Rock plat, now vacated.

stood. Farther on near the river the concrete outline of the depot can be found. The church camp building (A-frame) to the right has records and photographs of the old mill town.

The Black Rock post office was established in 1906, and a plat of twenty-two blocks was filed in 1910 by the C. K. Spaulding Logging Company. As the site of railroad logging operations and sawmilling, Black Rock attained a population of some six hundred persons in 1912. Look carefully around the grass and brush of the site for cast-off artifacts.

3.8   Black Rock to Falls City. Return via the same route to Falls City, also an old logging center and declining town. Turn left (east) and enter Falls City.

4.2   Falls City to State 223. Turn left (north) toward Dallas at the junction with State 223.

5.4   State 223 to Dallas. End of loop.

An old millpond, now unused.

EPILOGUE

Congratulations on completing the fourteen-hundred-mile tour of nearly 150 years of lumbering in western Oregon and Washington. The four loops of two hundred miles each in Washington and two long loops in Oregon represent only a selection of possible trips. Missed areas include the Columbia Gorge, Oregon Cascades, and Southern Oregon. Along each loop some interesting places were bypassed simply because they were a little out of the way, too small, or without information.

The boom-and-bust cycle of lumber-town growth forms a consistent theme throughout this journey. In explanation, analysts point to markets and competition, to technological change, to national economic health and, now, even to spotted owl protection. While all these conditions have an impact on lumber towns, the overriding, consistent, and fundamental characteristic is resource exhaustion. Until recent times, the Pacific Northwest's lumbering industry, based on exploitation of massive stands of virgin timber, bloated its local and regional capacities to effect a short-lived onetime condition. The forest may be a renewable resource, but an old-growth forest realistically is not. The forest economy will certainly continue to play a major role in the regional economic picture, but it will not be as large or dominating as it was in past times.

In retrospect, it is difficult to feel past experiences of place: struggles and aspirations, births and deaths, Christmas Eves and parades, routine and change, sounds and smells, homecomings and good-byes—in other words, the very grit of human experience. Yet, these things are there, in every little town or logging camp. They are the lumber ghosts.

INDEX

131